**Quick Start Guide**

CW00330581

The Essential
DIABETES DIET
COOKBOOK

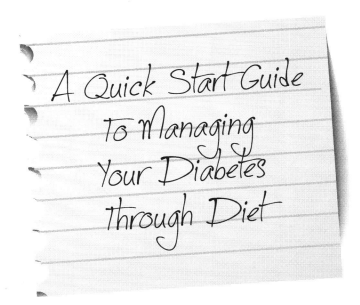

A Quick Start Guide To Managing Your Diabetes through Diet

Manage Your Sugar Levels, Feel Great and Increase Your Energy!

PLUS over 100 Diabetic Friendly Recipes

First published in 2014 by Erin Rose Publishing

Text and illustration copyright © 2014 Erin Rose Publishing

Design: Julie Anson

ISBN: 978-0-9928232-4-5

A CIP record for this book is available from the British Library.

DISCLAIMER: This book is for informational purposes only and not intended as a substitute for the medical advice, diagnosis or treatment of a medical physician or qualified healthcare provider. The reader should consult a physician before undertaking a new health care regimen and in all matters relating to his/her health, and particularly with respect to any symptoms that may require diagnosis or medical attention.

While every care has been taken in compiling the recipes for this book we cannot accept responsibility for any problems which arise as a result of preparing one of the recipes. The author and publisher disclaim responsibility for any adverse effects that may arise from the use or application of the recipes in this book. Some of the recipes in this book include nuts and eggs. If you have an egg or nut allergy it's important to avoid these. It is recommended that children, pregnant women, the elderly or anyone who has an immune system disorder avoids eating raw eggs included in any recipe

CONTENTS

Recipes

Breakfast

Lunch

Dinner

INTRODUCTION

If you are newly diagnosed with type 2 diabetes or pre-diabetes, and are confused by all the conflicting advice out there, then you're not alone. Nearly 350 million people worldwide have diabetes, and type 2 diabetes (diabetes mellitus) represents 90% of those cases. The number of people diagnosed with diabetes has skyrocketed, with the number of people in the UK more than doubling to 3 million since 1996. Statistics show 86 million Americans over the age of 20 had pre-diabetes in 2012, a rise of 7 million in only 2 years. And it's not showing signs of improving. What we have been doing hasn't been helping and despite diabetes becoming more common, it's still a big deal with serious health implications.

Perhaps you are a diabetic who was told to carry on eating as you normally would, and just take the medication. How has that been working for you? The advice for diabetics can be vague and some are told to eat plenty of starchy carbohydrates, but they increase insulin levels – that's a fact. If you are newly diagnosed with diabetes you may feel anxious about what this means in your daily life, which is understandable. Maybe it's time to quit doing the things which may have caused it. If your way of eating is adding to the problem, then it's time for change. It's time to try something different, because non-insulin dependent diabetes can worsen until you do become insulin dependent.

If you are ready to make a change and you're worried that you'll have to say goodbye to the foods you enjoy, don't be. We have recipes which won't leave you feeling deprived. If you, a friend, or a family member has diabetes and you are concerned about what to eat or even if you are looking for more variety, then help is at hand. We want you to love your food and enjoy healthier versions of your favourite dishes. In this **Quick Start Guide** we take a comprehensive approach with helpful, practical advice and plenty of delicious recipes for everyday cooking which are full of goodness. This book is intended to help you focus and get you started on a healthy diet.

What is Diabetes?

Diabetes is a chronic disease which occurs when either the pancreas does not produce enough insulin, or when the body cannot effectively use the insulin it does produce. Insulin is a hormone which regulates the body's blood glucose to maintain a healthy level, but with diabetes the body's blood glucose levels are dangerously high. The effects of raised blood glucose levels caused by uncontrolled diabetes can lead to serious damage particularly to the nerves and blood vessels.

What Causes Diabetes?

It varies depending on the type of diabetes as well as the person, but these add to the risk.

- Poor diet
- Family history of the disease
- Ethnicity – more prevalent in South Asian, African & Hispanic
- Increased age
- Being overweight
- Metabolic syndrome – a cluster of symptoms, including high blood sugar, high blood pressure, increased abdominal fat, high cholesterol and insulin resistance
- Insulin resistance is also linked to heart disease, dementia, fertility problems and PCOS

Despite the fact that diabetes can have very serious consequences, let's keep a positive attitude, because with the right dietary changes you can stabilise your blood glucose to reduce your reliance on medication. It can be an intimidating and disempowering experience to be told that you have a serious illness, but diabetes needn't be a sentence to poor health for the rest of your life. With dietary and lifestyle changes, you can make a difference and improve your health. If you have already tried unsuccessfully, don't be demoralised and don't give up. Keep going!

If you are thinking of cutting back on calories by eating diet foods, low-cal, sugar-free or fat-free options, drink supplements or ready meals designed for weight loss, think again. Ready meals, diet foods and drinks, touted as being fat-free or reduced fat, often contain high quantities of sugar to compensate for the lack of flavour.

The aim of this Quick Start Guide is not only to give you the information about what to eat but also how to make it, in simple easy-to-follow steps. The way forward includes reducing the intake of sugar, harmful fats and starchy carbohydrates like pasta, bread, potatoes, cakes and biscuits. But that includes a vast part of the 'normal' everyday diet for many of us, so now what do you eat? To stabilise blood glucose levels, you need to increase your intake of fresh vegetables, protein and good fats. In this book we tell you how to make mouth-watering meals and we have included 100 delicious, easy, guilt-free recipes which are not only packed with flavour but are good for you.

Take heart, take control and take action. It's understandable that if you've been feeling under par for a while and are now faced with the diagnosis of type 2 diabetes or pre-diabetes you feel you should just accept. Well now you can learn what you can do about it. When you have the knowledge, it gives you a choice; a very important one, to improve your blood glucose levels and safe guard your future wellbeing. There may not be a magic cure for diabetes, but more experts are standing up and saying that with a healthy diet and lifestyle improvements, type 2 diabetes can be reversible. And that's where you can make a difference. You have nothing to lose, except maybe some inches off your waist!

Managing And Preventing Type 2 Diabetes and Pre-diabetes. What Is It That Really Matters?

- Eating a healthy diet

- Getting a minimum of 30 minutes of exercise every day

- Maintaining a healthy weight

- Not smoking

- Restricting alcohol consumption

This Quick Start Guide takes care of the first item on the list. It provides a comprehensive approach, getting you up and running with practical advice, plus lots of delicious recipes to kick-start your healthy diet. It will help you get the most out of life and be the best that you can be. We want to guide you through the pit-falls and identify where you can make changes. And the best bit is; it's YOU that makes the difference!

You can achieve optimal health, whether you're on the cusp of developing diabetes or if you have been diagnosed with type 2 diabetes. Shake yourself down and move forward. Well done taking the first step. You're on your way!

Symptom Checker

If you have bought this book then the likelihood is that you, or a family member, have already been diagnosed with diabetes or pre-diabetes. But if not, and you are concerned about your health, you should consult your doctor if you have any of the following.

- Increased or constant thirst

- Excessive urination, especially at night

- Abnormal fatigue

- Unexplained weight loss, not as a result of dieting

- Increased appetite and feeling hungry despite eating

- Blurred vision

While being overweight is a risk factor for developing this disease, other risk factors such as genetics and diet also play a role. Many overweight people never develop type 2 diabetes and many people with type 2 diabetes are not overweight.

You may have had no symptoms before you were diagnosed or you could have been experiencing some pretty horrible symptoms such as unexplained anxiety, light-headedness, extreme fatigue and the inability to lose weight due to insulin resistance. This book isn't intended for medical diagnosis, but to provide you with information to increase your awareness and help you to take steps towards better health. If you are diabetic, you should consult your doctor before making extreme dietary changes.

Pre-diabetes

Pre-diabetes, where blood glucose levels are border-line, is a precursor to type 2 diabetes. But if it is picked up early, it can mark a turning point, where implementing positive changes can prevent the condition from getting worse.

The Effects Of Uncontrolled Diabetes

Diabetes increases the risk of circulation problems, ulcers, nerve damage, diabetic retinopathy, kidney disease, heart disease and strokes. To avoid complications, changing your diet and getting plenty of exercise should be an integral part of your plan. Work with your doctor, explain that you want to make changes and discuss your medication requirements.

Should Diabetics Eat Sugar?

Sugar isn't healthy in anyone's diet. Excess sugar can result in insulin resistance and metabolic syndrome which leads to diabetes. Furthermore, added sugar and fructose can lead to high cholesterol and non-alcoholic fatty liver disease. However one concern is that restricting sugar and carbohydrates can result in hypoglycaemia, which is when the blood sugar falls too low. If a diabetic's blood sugar drops too low, eating a sweet snack may be essential to bring blood glucose levels up to a normal level. If you find you are getting hypoglycaemia seek your doctor's advice.

Cutting Back On The Carbs

Many of us reach for a carbohydrate-rich meal or snack when we're hungry, or as comfort food. However, your serving size should be no more than ¼ of a plate (1 cup) of healthy, wholegrain carbs. Be aware that potatoes elevate blood glucose quicker than other starchy vegetables which are broken down more slowly, providing a healthier gradual release of energy.

Fructose & Artificial Sweeteners

The harmful effects of sugar are well known. But what about our consumption of natural, and apparently healthy sugar – fructose? Fructose or fruit sugar consumption is one of the top reasons why the 'healthy' eaters in our population have become frustrated with their results; from craving sweet treats to increasing abdominal fat. Fruit is great and packed full of nutrients, but we need to be careful of the sugar content. Sweet tasting things are seductive and make us crave more. It's thought to be healthy to have a large glass of pure orange juice at breakfast time, an apple juice with lunch and dinner, but this 'healthy' habit delivers an overwhelming amount of sugar.

One glass of fresh apple juice has 6 ½ teaspoons of sugar, compared to a fizzy soft drink which has around a 5 ½ teaspoons. The problem is, fructose is metabolised in small amounts by the liver, aided by fruit's own fibre. However many of us regularly consume vast quantities which are harmful and are shown to result in a fatty liver. Concentrated fruit juices have most of their fibre removed, making it a fast form of liquid sugar. Rather than being used immediately as fuel, fructose is converted and stored as fat.

Aside from the health concerns about artificial sweeteners it's been discovered that they affect the body's ability to gauge how much has been consumed. At the University of California, San Diego, researchers found that our brains respond to sweet flavours by producing signals to eat more of it. By providing a sweet taste, without any calories, it causes us to crave more sweet foods and drinks. Being tempted by sweet tasting things is a bad idea when you are kick starting a healthy diet!

Many of us have ditched the chocolate bars, sweet fizzy drinks and reached for an apparently healthy muesli bar and a large glass of pure orange juice instead, but we've just leapt from the frying pan into the fire, in terms of the sugar content. Let's differentiate between naturally occurring fructose in whole fruits and vegetables, and that which is processed and added to food products, such as high fructose corn syrup. People often opt for natural sweet-eners like honey or maple syrup or agave syrup which is a popular sweetener. Agave syrup, which is from natural sugar, is not the sweet calorie-free dream it was thought to be. It has been cleared of all fibre, processed and concen-trated and is extremely high in fructose. It can contain anything from 75% to 92% fructose. The quantity is actually higher than high-fructose corn syrup, which has 55% and has had a good deal of negative publicity. It's also much higher than white table sugar, which is 50% fructose thus making agave syrup more harmful than either high fructose corn syrup or white refined sugar.

Sweeteners, with the exception of stevia, which we'll get to in a minute, have been controversial since the 1970's and have been linked to a high Body Mass Index, chronic illnesses and cancer. Studies produced conflicting results on the safety of the chemical sweeteners which are added to sweets, diet foods, low-calorie soft drinks, and medicines. Artificial chemical sweeteners such as saccharin, sucralose and aspartame are made by a highly-industrial process. They have virtually no calories or glycemic index, and they've been linked to chronic illnesses in numerous studies. Yet the outcomes of these studies are inconclusive. In the meantime they are still being added to our everyday food, despite reports that they are harmful.

Included in this book are recipes which use stevia to give you the safest option for a sweetener. Stevia or sweet leaf is derived from the South American Stevia Rebaudiana plant. It won't elevate your blood glucose and doesn't contain calories.

Know Your Enemy: The Good & Bad Fats

For decades we've been told that the staurated fat found in dairy, meat and plants are bad for us and to avoid it or be at risk of developing high cholesterol and heart disease, but more recently there has been a swing in this opinion. The obsession with reduced fat products has reached far and wide; from skinny lattes to low fat yogurt and reduced fat biscuits. Manufacturers have added sugar to products where the fat has been removed, to compensate for the reduction in taste.

Well, we've followed the advice and results are in. But they're not good! Despite everything, the rates of obesity have rocketed. Research is now not supporting the idea that saturated fat is as harmful as we believed. Instead, the evidence is piling up against sugar. We've reduced our fat intake, increased our sugar consumption and here we are today with rampant obesity and soaring rates of diabetes. However, change is on the horizon. This swing has lead to doctors speaking out, saying it's a myth that saturated fat is linked to heart disease. In fact 75% of patients admitted to hospital suffering a heart attack have normal cholesterol levels.

Dairy products are high in saturated fat, but they are also high in vitamins A and D. Furthermore a fatty acid which is found in dairy products is related to high levels of good cholesterol and reduced insulin resistance. Fat actually makes us feel full – it's rich in energy and because of this we consume less calories. We reach a fill level, whereas sugar perpetuates hunger with the desire for more sugar and powerful cravings.

More and more studies are showing that people achieve greater weight loss on diets which are low in carbohydrate rather than low in fat. So it seems saturated fat has been wrongly accused. But, like anything, fats consumed to excess will cause weight gain, but our energy has to come from somewhere and natural fats are a form of sustenance. Moderation is the key. Our mistrust of saturated fats is ingrained, but the real danger is the artificial trans-fats or trans-fatty acids. They are formed by adding hydrogen to vegetable oils during the industrial process. Hydrogenated oil has a longer shelf life, so it doesn't need to be changed as often as other oils, making it commercially cheaper. Hydrogenated and partially hydrogenated fat can be found in bread, cakes, pies, crackers, frozen products, fries and non-dairy margarine. They raise LDL (bad) cholesterol, lower HDL (good) cholesterol, makes blood platelets stickier leading to clots. They are also inflammatory and can lead to heart disease, strokes and diabetes.

What Can I Do To Help My Diabetes

Early diagnosis is important. Treatment of diabetes involves lowering blood glucose to reduce the risk of complications. This goes for pre-diabetes and staving off full blown type 2 diabetes.

You can take positive action:

- Quitting smoking helps avoid complications of diabetes.

- Adopt a healthy diet, low in sugar and starchy foods which contain little fibre. Carbohydrate intake should be from wholegrain foods.

- A serving of complex carbohydrate, around 1 cup, alongside a meal consisting of protein, vegetables and beneficial fat will help negate the effects that a carbohydrate would have if eaten on its own.

- Eat some protein at every meal or as a snack.

- Get plenty of fibre from fresh vegetables.

- Avoid all trans-fats.

- Avoid starchy or sugary food. It elevates blood sugar and will result in you feeling hungry fairly quickly making you more likely to overeat

- Eat at least every 4 to 6 hours. Little and often is better.

- Don't miss meals! That is really important. You need regular fuel.

- Only eat fruit in its entirety i.e. including the fruit's fibre because the fibre it contains delays absorption of carbohydrates and sugar.

- Instead of hitting a sugary snack opt for a healthy fat option. Coconut, avocado, walnuts, pecans, macadamia nuts, sunflower and pumpkin seeds, eggs, flaxseeds, olives, oily fish like salmon, mackerel, trout and sardines.

- Keep fruit intake low. Maximum of 2 pieces a day.

- Don't eat after dinner which should ideally be early evening.

What triggers blood sugar spikes in one person doesn't always cause the same reaction in another. Using a glucose meter, and testing blood glucose levels 2 hours after a meal you may be able to work out what food is having a greater effect on your sugar levels. Careful monitoring is important and re-member, if you are ill your blood glucose levels can also be elevated. Keeping a record of what you have eaten, and your resulting glucose levels will enable you to monitor if something is having a particularly adverse affect on you. If it is, then you can avoid it.

You may already be in the habit of testing regularly, particularly if your health-care team has advised you when to test, so that you can keep a close check on things and look out for falling or escalating blood glucose levels.

Keep A Food Diary

Most of us think we eat a lot less than we actually do, so it's worth keeping a food diary and keeping a record of what you eat. You can see repeating patterns and identify where unhealthy foods are creeping in.

Although starchy vegetables, like squash, pumpkin and carrots are considered high in carbohydrate, they still very low compared to refined processed prod-ucts. Plus they have the essential benefit of containing valuable amounts of fibre, vitamins and minerals. What affects one person may not affect another to the same degree, so keep a record of what affects you. Refined carbohy-drates like cakes, biscuits and white bread not only elevate blood sugar but they are very low in nutrients and fibre.

What Can I Eat?

Don't Eat These:

Any food containing sugar: read all labels – see specific section.

- Avoid starchy carbohydrates; pasta, corn, bread and white flour products. Wholegrain is better.

- Avoid all products containing sugar, glucose syrup, fructose, high fructose corn syrup, agave nectar, honey, syrup, jams, jellies and maple syrup – read all labels. (See the section on how to read labels.)

- Avoid hydrogenated or partially hydrogenated vegetable oils. They are found in margarine, fried food, factory produced cakes and biscuits.

- Breakfast cereals where some form of sugar is added – that's virtually all of them, even granola & muesli.

- Cakes, biscuits, muffins, muesli, cereal bars and cookies.

- Avoid all fizzy and sugary drinks, including diet drinks with artificial sweeteners.

- Avoid chocolate, sweets and candy – even if they are diet or low-calorie.

- Avoid dried fruit, including dates, apricots, raisins, bananas, sultanas, apples, mango, pineapple, figs.

- Avoid pure or concentrated fruit juices.

- Beware of ready-made sauces like sweet & sour, curry, relish, ketchup and barbeque sauce – they generally have sugar added.

- Alcohol consumption. Keep it between zero and low.

- Don't add sugar to tea and coffee.

Do Eat These:

Clear away all those temptations from your cupboards and stock up on what you can eat – wholesome nutritious low-sugar, low-carb, high-fibre food. If it's green, you can go ahead and load up. Eat some protein with every meal. It staves off hunger and has little effect on blood sugar. Make sure you have lots of high protein snacks available.

- Chicken, turkey, pork, lamb and beef.
- Seafood: prawns, salmon, trout, sardines, herring and mackerel (all oily fish are good).
- Nuts (uncoated) e.g. Brazils, hazelnuts, almonds, cashews and pecans.
- Seeds e.g. sunflower, sesame and pumpkin.
- Brown rice, quinoa.
- Vegetables: Avocado, cauliflower, broccoli, kale, pumpkin, sweet potato, onions, carrots, watercress, celery, peppers, tomatoes, lettuce, spinach, courgette, green beans, Brussels sprouts, turnip, bean sprouts and pak choi.
- Cheese.
- Pulses and legumes.
- Eggs.
- Plain unflavoured yogurt – you can easily add your own flavour.
- Nut butters: peanut, almond, cashew.
- Tinned fish, such as tuna or sardines.
- Herby teas and plenty of water
- Low sugar fruit like raspberries, blackberries, strawberries, rhubarb, lime, lemons. (Fig, mango and grapes are high in fructose).
- Peppermint chamomile, green tea & herbal teas (fruit teas – check sugar content).
- Coconut flakes.
- Coconut oil, olive oil, ground nut oils.
- Fresh herbs and spices, ginger, garlic vinegar, soy sauce.
- Cooked/sliced meets eg. cooked chicken, prawns or ham to nibble on.

Quinoa, pronounced 'keen wah' is a very nutritious, high protein grain which is packed with goodness. It really is a wonder food to help break the starchy carbohydrate cravings for white bread or cakes.

Avoid too much fruit. Limit it to 2 pieces a day, or some people avoid it completely. It sounds harsh, because fruit has so many benefits, but it could tempt you to have more fruit or even sugary snacks. Some of the recipes included in this book do have fruit in them and it's probably best to eat these in moderation.

You might want to avoid high sugar fruits like mango and pineapple, in favour of raspberries and blackberries which have around a quarter of the fructose content. That way you'll be able to keep fruit in your diet without having too much sugar. However, having a couple of pieces of whole fruit is nowhere near as harmful as adding refined sugars and fibre-free fructose like concentrated fruit juices.

Fruit is packed with nutrients and importantly it's a real treat to the taste buds. Food should be enjoyable. The best way to eat fruit is in its whole, natural state, as the fibre will slow down the absorption of the sugar. Concentrated and pure fruit juices, are basically liquid fructose and they will trigger spikes in blood sugar.

Food which is sold as 'diabetic' and "dietetic" generally offers no special benefit. They just cost a lot more. Make sure sweet treats come in small portions and save them for special occasions. Instead, focus on healthy foods.

How Much Is Too Much?
Carbohydrate Quantities Per 100g Serving

Medium carbohydrate content – less than 30g

Low carbohydrate content – less than 15g

Very low carbohydrate – less than 3g

Approximately 1 cup or ¼ plateful is usually sufficient. However, everyone's tolerance for carbohydrate is different and this is only a guide. Monitoring your blood sugar after eating a carbohydrate based meal will help gauge your tolerance if your glucose levels rise substantially.

As a quick guide, here are the carbohydrate contents of some foods to help you identify where you wish to restrict your intake. Try and stay under 30g of carbohydrate in one meal. Always eat protein at every meal, to offset the effects of the carb and have plenty of fibre from fresh vegetables as it slows down absorption. If you are insulin resistant or trying to lose weight you may wish to reduce your carb intake further.

Food	Carbohydrate Content Per 100g
Table sugar	100g
Honey	82g
Raisins	79g
Dates	75g
Pasta	75g
Tortilla chips	73g
Oats	66g
White bread	73g
Chocolate	61g
Wholemeal bread	49g
French fries	41g
White rice	28g
Brown rice	23g
Quinoa	21g
Sweet potato	20g
Sweet corn	19g
Apple	14g
Raspberries	12g
Brazil nuts	12g
Carrots	10g
Avocado	9g
Celeriac	9g

Butternut squash..8.3g

Pumpkin..6g

Olives 6g

Mozzarella 2.2g

Cheddar cheese...1.3g

Spinach 3.6g

Baby sweet corn..3.1g

Lettuce 2.9g

Eggs 1.1g

Prawns 0.9g

Chicken 0g

Olive oil.. 0g

How To Read The Labels

So you pick up a low-sugar or diet ready-meal and you think it's got to be healthy, right? Wrong! When you look at the label you could discover there are hidden sugars. If you look for trans-fats don't be fooled by the word 'vegetable' in the title and think that it's healthy. Below is a list of names for fats and sugars. It's best to avoid these.

Trans-Fats

- Hydrogenated vegetable oil

- Partially hydrogenated vegetable oil

- Hydrogenated saturated fat

- Partially hydrogenated saturated fat

- Partially hydrogenated coconut oil

- Partially hydrogenated palm oil

- Hydrogenated soybean oil

Are you seeing a pattern here? If it says partially hydrogenated or hydrogenated – don't eat it! It may not be listed in the nutrition data of the label, but make sure and check the ingredients list too.

Note: In the U.S. only food with more than 0.5g of trans-fat actually needs to have it declared on the label. Your product can be marketed as being trans-fat free, but still contain trans-fat. Very deceptive! Small amounts add up, especially if you regularly eat it in large quantities. In fact the FDA has now determined that partially hydrogenated and hydrogenated oil is not now 'generally recognised as safe' and they want it banned.

SUGAR

- Invert sugar syrup
- Brown sugar
- Cane sugar
- Cane juice crystals
- Dextrin
- Dextrose
- Glucose
- Glucose syrup
- Sucrose
- Fructose
- Fructose syrup
- Maltodextrin
- Barley malt
- Beet sugar
- Corn syrup
- High Fructose Corn Syrup
- Caramel
- Date sugar
- Palm sugar
- Malt syrup
- Refiners syrup
- Fruit juice concentrate
- Carob syrup
- Golden syrup
- Refiners syrup
- Ethylmaltol

Get Prepared And Get Started!

Stock up on tasty, healthy ingredients and empty your cupboards of un-healthy temptations. If you haven't already, start cutting out those obviously sugar laden foods, the fizzy drinks, sweets, cakes, chocolate. It'll make it easier when you cut out those hidden sugars and reduce your cravings. As your preparation takes shape, and you're kicking out those excess carbs and unhealthy fats and sugars, don't set yourself a start date. It's like building a wall to jump over. Don't make it hard for yourself. Easy does it. Once your cupboards are re-stocked and you've had a look at some recipes it's time to get started. Remember, to consult your doctor before making radical changes to your diet/lifestyle as it may involve careful monitoring or an adjustment to medication.

What To Expect

So let's not sugar coat this! If you've been eating what is classed today as a normal diet, you've probably been consuming way too much salt, sugar and harmful fats. Therefore, expect some craving. These can vary in degree, depending on your current diet. Diminish any thoughts of your food temp-tations, and do something else. So, while you are adjusting, distract yourself, think of something else, get some exercise, and drink plenty of water. Taking a walk will keep you away from the kitchen!

Top Tips To Make It Easy

If you get sugar cravings and there is a likelihood that you will, don't be tempted to reach for a sweet or starchy snack. Opt for a protein option and kick sugar cravings to the curb. The early days are by far the hardest, but once healthy eating has become your new normal, you will no longer crave the unhealthy things. Distraction is one of the best ways to overcome cravings. Literally, get up and do something. Think about something else.

- To avoid a mid-morning lull, start your day with a protein packed breakfast like eggs and bacon.

- Watch your starchy food and carbohydrate consumption, especially flour products. Keep it low.

- Snack on coconut chips, Brazil nuts, cashews, pecans, macadamia nuts, pumpkin and sunflower seeds, olives, small cubes of cheese and chicken.

- Have a teaspoon of peanut butter (sugar-free of course!)

- At dinner time, replace starchy high carbohydrates like pasta and bread with lots of fresh vegetables and you'll feel less hungry and sluggish.

- Drink plenty of water!

- Avoid dried fruit (it's loaded with fructose) – make your snacks protein based instead.

- A tub of olives is a handy snack, which is packed with healthy satisfying fats.

- Plan easy meals in advance so as to avoid ravenously bolting for a stodgy meal.

- Never miss a meal.

- Eating five meals/snacks a day is best, but watch your portion sizes. Eat little and often.

- Prepare some cucumber water. Steep slices of cucumber and a few mint leaves in a large jug of water. Store it in the fridge and serve it with ice and lemon.

- Get some exercise – walking, swimming and cycling can help.

- Pamper yourself with a bath, perhaps add magnesium (Epsom) salts to help you relax.

- Get busy preparing some tasty meals and treats for the fridge or freezer. That way you'll have a store of healthy food, so you won't be tempted by a quick fix. Reward yourself with something you've prepared and store the rest in the freezer.

- Get plenty of rest and sleep.

- Carry on-the-go snacks for a quick bit of sustenance.

- Don't criticise yourself for giving in to temptation occasionally, just carry on eating well and treat it as a minor glitch. Always move on from your slip-ups! Start afresh the next day.

- Acknowledge your achievements. If you can manage it for one day, you can manage it for a week and if you can do that you can keep it going. Once you start feeling better, the temporary challenges will have subsided. Treat it as a lifestyle change and make healthy your new normal.

Monitoring Your Progress & Adding Treats

Once you've got the hang of what you can and can't eat and you have a selection of your favourite ingredients, you can play around with them and experiment. You're bound to find your own staples which are handy and quick to prepare.

If you're being pretty strict with yourself and been avoiding fruit, you may want to add it into your diet after a month or so. Keep it to a maximum of 2 pieces a day. Maybe try an occasional treat. The dessert and chocolate recipes in this book are included as a treat and are to be eaten in moderation. Don't over indulge. Keep testing your blood sugar after a meal. The other thing to be wary of is the stimulated taste buds from sweet things. We don't want your taste buds longing for similar things which are much higher in sugar. At the end of a meal, you could try snacking on nuts or cheese instead.

Here's The Best Bit! Mouth Watering Recipes.

The recipes contained in this book are sugar-free, delicious and easy. The section for tasty snacks and delicious desserts is at the back. We don't want you to feel deprived when you make healthy changes. On the contrary, by making healthy changes you'll adjust to the more subtle flavours in your food. Experimenting and finding out what works for you is the key.

Once your kitchen cupboards are stocked with what you like, you can play around with the recipes and find your favourites. Get creative and make it easier. Put the right kind of temptation in your way: include in your diet something which you can really look forward to like kale chips or seasoned nuts. There are plenty of suggestions to beat those cravings which can threaten your new healthy habits.

Recipes

BREAKFAST

In Chinese Medicine, it's understood that each organ in the body has a time of high and low functioning, alternating in two hour cycles. The stomach's peak of energy is between 7am and 9am, which is the optimal time to refuel. Avoid a mid-morning lull and start your day with a protein breakfast, even if it's only a couple of quickly scrambled eggs. Smoothies made in a blender are a wonderfully nutritious start, but watch those fruit juices where the liquid is extracted without the bulky fibre. Remember, we want the fibre to slow down absorption of sugars. Have some protein with every meal to make sure you don't get hungry. Protein has much less of an effect on blood glucose than carbohydrates.

LUNCH

Most of us find it easier to put together a healthy meal but we can make life easier by making large batches at a time; leftovers are a good thing. A quick warm up meal the next day or one which is stored in the freezer can be invaluable for throwing together a tasty meal. You can stir up leftover meat and veggies in a pan, add beaten eggs or cheese and make a really satisfying omelette.

DINNER

To keep your carbohydrate intake down, substitute mashed potatoes for vegetable alternatives like celeriac or sweet potato mash. A lower carbohydrate intake will help prevent your blood glucose from spiking, reduce your cravings for stodgy food. Make extra and store it for when time and imagination is lacking. Keep all leftovers and chill or freeze them. They'll provide the basics for another nutritious meal.

SNACKS, SWEET TREATS & DESSERTS

If you have a sweet tooth then this may be the section you skip to. As well as dessert recipes we have included snack options to give you something to nibble on in between meals or if you get an attack of the after-dinner munchies when you are likely to raid the cupboards thinking 'what can I eat now?'. Our chocolate recipes contain 100% cocoa powder and stevia, a natural sweetener, giving you the fabulous chocolate hit but keeping it sugar-free. However, a note of caution; we know sweet tasting things can give your taste buds a hunger for other sweet treats. It could be a real test of your will-power not to eat other desserts which aren't sugar free. Therefore, only eat these in moderation occasionally, not instead of a meal. We want you to carry on your healthy eating but we know how important it is to enjoy your food. If the temptation is too great, stave off those cravings by reverting to protein and a nice cheese board. Good luck and happy, healthy eating!

BREAKFAST

Ham & Tomato Breakfast Pots

Ingredients

75g (3oz) ham, finely chopped
4 large eggs
1 small tomato, sliced
1 tablespoon fresh basil, finely chopped
4 teaspoons crème fraiche

SERVES
4

Method

Lightly grease 4 ramekin dishes then line the bases and sides with ham. Crack an egg into each ramekin. Top each one with a slice of tomato. Add a teaspoon of crème fraiche and a sprinkle of basil. Place in the oven at 180C/350F for 16 to 18 minutes for soft yolks, or if you want the eggs set completely leave them in longer. Season and serve.

Baked Eggs
& Smoked Salmon

Ingredients

4 large eggs
25g (1oz) spinach, stalks removed
75g (3oz) smoked salmon slices
1 teaspoon olive oil
1 tablespoon crème fraiche
1 garlic clove, crushed
Freshly ground black pepper

**SERVES
4**

Method

Heat the olive oil in a pan and add the garlic. When the garlic starts to soften, add the spinach. Cook for 2-3 minutes until the spinach has wilted. Line the bases and sides of 4 ramekin dishes with smoked salmon. Divide the spinach and the garlic between the ramekin dishes then break an egg into each one. Spoon some crème fraiche over each egg and sprinkle with black pepper. Place the ramekins in a preheated oven at 220C/425F for 15 minutes, until the eggs are set. Serve and enjoy.

Meatloaf Minis

Ingredients

8 rashers (strips of bacon)
225g (½ lb) bacon, chopped
450g (1lb) minced beef (ground beef)
4 tablespoons chives, chopped
1 tablespoon fresh parsley, chopped
2 cloves of garlic, finely chopped
½ teaspoon nutmeg
½ teaspoon cinnamon
60ml (2 floz or ¼ cup) coconut milk
Freshly ground black pepper

MAKES 8

Method

Place the minced beef, chopped bacon, garlic, cinnamon, nutmeg, parsley, chives and coconut milk in a large bowl and combine. Season with pepper. Completely line the hollows of an 8-hole muffin tin with the strips of bacon, trimming if necessary. Spoon the meatloaf mixture on top of the bacon. Bake the mini meatloaves in the oven at 200C/400F for 30 minutes. Remove them from the muffin tin and serve.

Cheese & Broccoli Mini Omelettes

SERVES 4

Ingredients

4 large eggs
50g (2oz or ⅓ cup) Cheddar cheese, grated (shredded)
100g (4oz or ⅔ cup) broccoli florets
Freshly ground black pepper

Method

Place the broccoli in a steamer and cook for about 5 minutes until tender. Break it into smaller pieces and set aside. In a separate bowl, whisk the eggs then add the grated cheese and black pepper. Add the broccoli and mix well. Lightly grease a muffin tin. Pour in the egg and broccoli mixture. Bake in the oven at 180C/350F for around 20 minutes until the eggs are set. Serve immediately.

Soft Eggs & Asparagus Dippers

SERVES 2

Ingredients

4 large eggs
1 bunch of asparagus
Sea salt
Freshly ground black pepper

Method

Place the eggs in a saucepan of boiling water and cook for 4 minutes. Meanwhile, steam the asparagus for 3 to 4 minutes, until tender. Drain the eggs and place them in egg cups. Cut the tops off, season with salt and pepper. Serve a few spears of asparagus on a plate next to it. The asparagus can be used to dip into the runny yolks and are a great healthy alternative to toast.

Cheese & Olive Frittata

Ingredients

75g (3oz or ½ cup) black olives
4 large eggs
8 cherry tomatoes, halved
100g (3 ½ oz or 1 cup) Cheddar cheese, grated (shredded)
1 tablespoon olive oil
Sea salt
Freshly ground black pepper

SERVES
2

Method

Cut the olives into half, removing all stones. Crack the eggs into a bowl and whisk. Season with salt and pepper. Heat the oil in a small frying pan and pour in the egg mixture. Add in the tomatoes and olives, cut side up. Sprinkle with cheese. Cook until the mixture completely sets. Place the frittata under a hot grill for 3 minutes. The eggs should be set and the cheese slightly golden. Gently remove from the pan. Cut into slices and serve immediately.

Baked Eggs & Beef Tomato

Ingredients

4 beef tomatoes or other large tomatoes
200g (7oz or 1 cup) brown rice, cooked
4 teaspoons pesto
4 large eggs
Pinch of salt

SERVES 4

Method

Cut the tops off the tomatoes. Scoop out the centres and discard. Sprinkle with a little salt and place, cut-side down, on paper towel for 15 minutes to drain. Preheat the oven to 180°C/350F. Stuff the rice into the tomatoes filling to 1-2cm before the top. You need to allow space for the egg. Add a teaspoon of pesto to the rice. Use crumpled foil to make a nest for each tomato and place on a baking tray. Break an egg into each tomato, and bake with the tomato tops for about 15 to 20 minutes or until cooked. Serve immediately.

Cucumber & Apple Smoothie

Ingredients
- ½ apple
- ½ cucumber
- ½ carrot
- 1 tablespoon sunflower seeds
- 2 teaspoons sesame seeds
- Handful of spinach

SERVES
1

Method

Place all the ingredients into a blender with a cup of water. Blitz until smooth. You can add a little extra water if you don't want it too thick.

Spinach & Carrot Smoothie

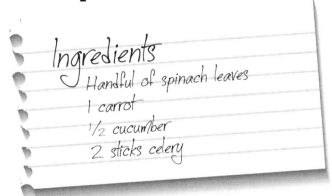

Ingredients
- Handful of spinach leaves
- 1 carrot
- ½ cucumber
- 2 sticks celery

SERVES
1

Method

Put all the ingredients into a blender with a cup of water, and blitz until smooth. You can add ice to some blenders which will make your smoothie really refreshing.

Blueberry & Coconut Smoothie

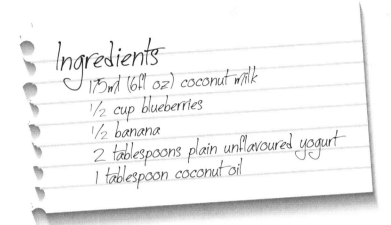

Ingredients
- 175ml (6fl oz) coconut milk
- 1/2 cup blueberries
- 1/2 banana
- 2 tablespoons plain unflavoured yogurt
- 1 tablespoon coconut oil

SERVES
1

Method

Toss all of the ingredients into a blender. Blitz until creamy. Pour and enjoy!

Green Glory Smoothie

Ingredients
- 1/2 avocado
- Handful of spinach leaves
- Handful of kale
- 1 apple
- Juice from 1/4 lemon
- 2 tablespoon pumpkin seeds

SERVES
1

Method

Put all the ingredients into a blender with just enough water to cover the ingredients. Blitz until smooth. You can add more lemon juice for extra zing.

Almond Pancakes

Ingredients

2 eggs
60ml (2fl oz or 1/4 cup) water
125g (4 1/2 oz) almond flour
1 teaspoon baking powder
2 teaspoons coconut oil
Pinch of cinnamon

SERVES
1

Method

Put the eggs in a bowl, whisk them and set aside. Combine the dry ingredients in a separate bowl and stir in the beaten eggs. Add the water and mix until you have a smooth batter. Heat a little coconut oil in a frying pan. Pour a small amount of mixture into the pan to make small pancakes. Cook the pancakes until golden brown. Serve with a generous sprinkling of cinnamon.

Coconut Pancakes

SERVES 1

Ingredients

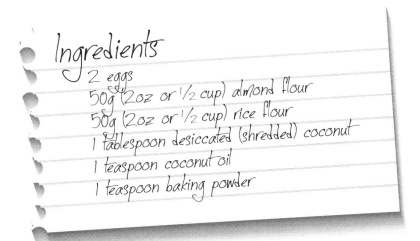

2 eggs
50g (2oz or ½ cup) almond flour
50g (2oz or ½ cup) rice flour
1 tablespoon desiccated (shredded) coconut
1 teaspoon coconut oil
1 teaspoon baking powder

Method

Whisk the eggs and set aside. Add the dry ingredients to a large bowl. Stir the whisked eggs into the dry ingredients, mixing until the batter is smooth. Heat the coconut oil in a frying pan. Spoon some of the mixture into the pan. Smaller pancakes work best, as being a gluten free recipe, the pancakes are very soft and light. When bubbles appear, turn them over to finish cooking.

Pancake Toppers

Try one of the options below or experiment to find your favourite.

Banana & raspberry
Blueberry & apple
Blackberry & orange

To make the pancake toppings, just place a small portion of your chosen fruit into a blender then pour the sauce over pancakes. You can add a squeeze of lemon juice or a little cinnamon to jazz it up.

LUNCH

Fennel & Broccoli Soup

Ingredients

1 fennel bulb
2 heads of broccoli, chopped
1 tablespoon dill
1 tablespoon fresh parsley
1 tablespoon crème fraiche (optional)
Freshly ground black pepper

SERVES
4-6

Method

Place the broccoli and fennel in enough water to cover them and bring to the boil.
Simmer for 7 minutes until they are soft but tender. Add the parsley and dill. Transfer
to a food processor and blend until smooth. Stir in the crème fraiche (optional).
Season and serve.

Cauliflower Soup

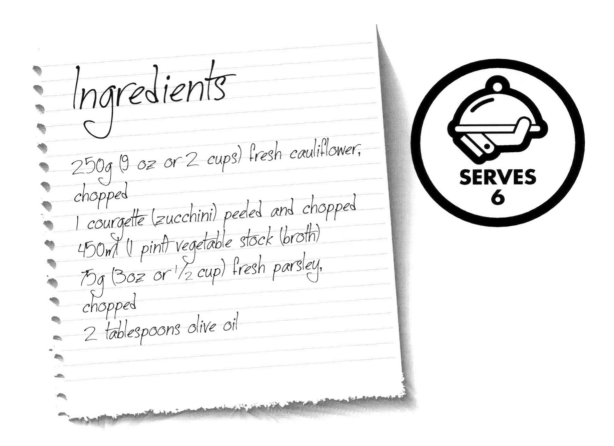

Ingredients

250g (9 oz or 2 cups) fresh cauliflower, chopped

1 courgette (zucchini) peeled and chopped

450ml (1 pint) vegetable stock (broth)

75g (3oz or ½ cup) fresh parsley, chopped

2 tablespoons olive oil

SERVES 6

Method

Heat the olive oil in a large saucepan and add the cauliflower and courgette (zucchini). Cook for around 5 minutes, stirring occasionally. Add the stock (broth), and simmer gently for 15 minutes. Pour the soup into a blender, add the parsley and blitz until smooth. Return the soup to the saucepan and gently simmer for 5 minutes to heat it through. It can be served hot or cold.

Chicken & Vegetable Soup

Ingredients

SERVES 4

225g (8oz) chicken, cubed
1 courgette (zucchini), chopped
2 stalks of asparagus, chopped
2 medium carrots, chopped
1 stalk of celery, chopped
3 tablespoons fresh parsley
900ml (1 ½ pints) chicken stock (broth)
1 tablespoons olive oil
Sea salt
Freshly ground black pepper

Method

Heat the olive oil in a frying pan. Add the chicken and cook for 5 minutes. Place the chicken and stock (broth) in a large saucepan. Cook for 5 minutes. Add the courgette (zucchini), carrot, celery, asparagus and parsley. Continue cooking for around 20 minutes, until the vegetables are soft. Season and serve.

Squash & Ginger Soup

Ingredients

1 butternut squash, peeled, de-seeded and chopped

900mls (1 ½ pts) of vegetable stock

4cm fresh root ginger, chopped

1 medium onion, chopped

120ml (4fl oz or ½ cup) coconut milk

1 tablespoon olive oil

SERVES 4

Method

In a large saucepan, heat the olive oil and add the onion. Cook for 4 minutes or until the onion is soft. Add to the saucepan the squash, ginger and stock. Bring to the boil then reduce the heat and simmer for 15 minutes. Transfer the soup to a blender and process until smooth. Stir in the coconut milk. Return the soup to the heat and warm it through before serving.

Avocado & Coriander (Cilantro) Soup

Ingredients

1 large avocado
Juice from ½ lime
900ml (1 ½ pints or 4 cups) chicken stock (broth)
250ml (½ pint or 1 ¼ cups) crème fraiche
2 tablespoons of coriander (cilantro), chopped

SERVES
4

Method

Cut the avocado in half, remove the stone and discard then scoop out the flesh. Place the avocado in a blender. Add 4 tablespoons of the crème fraiche and blitz until smooth. In a saucepan, heat the chicken stock (broth) and add the remaining crème fraiche. Add the lime juice to the avocado mixture and mix. Gently stir in the avocado mixture to the chicken stock, keeping it on a low heat until it is combined. Add the coriander (cilantro), season and serve.

Stilton & Watercress Soup

Ingredients

600ml (1pt or 2 ½ cups) vegetable stock (broth)
225g (8oz or 5 cups) watercress
150g (5oz or 1 cup) Stilton or other blue cheese
150ml (5fl oz or ¾ cup) natural yogurt (unflavoured)

SERVES 4

Method

Pour the vegetable stock (broth) into a large pan and bring to the boil. Remove and discard any thick stalks of watercress then add it to the pan. Gently simmer for around 3 minutes or until the watercress is tender. Break up the cheese and sprinkle in the pan. Simmer for 1-2 minutes until the cheese has melted. Pour the soup into a blender and blitz until smooth. Pour the soup back into the pan. Stir in the yogurt and heat gently. Serve and enjoy.

Kale & Chickpea (Garbanzo Beans) Soup

Ingredients

150g (5oz or 1 cup) chickpeas (garbanzo beans)

150g (5oz or 1 cup) curly kale

1 onion, peeled and finely chopped

1 carrot, peeled and diced

400ml (1 pint) vegetable stock (broth)

1/2 teaspoon tomato puree (paste)

1/2 teaspoon basil

1 clove garlic, crushed

1 teaspoon olive oil

SERVES 4

Method

Heat the olive oil in a large saucepan and add the garlic, together with the carrots and onions. Stir for 2 to 3 minutes on a medium heat. Add the vegetable stock and bring to the boil. Reduce the heat and cook for 15 minutes. In a food processor, blend half of the chickpeas and add them to the soup. Add the kale, the remaining chickpeas, tomato puree and basil. Stir and cook for 10 minutes. Season and serve into bowls. If you prefer your soup smooth, pour it into a food processor and blend until smooth.

Smoked Mackerel Pate

Ingredients

4 smoked mackerel fillets, skin removed
8 tablespoons crème fraiche
1/2 teaspoon fresh dill, finely chopped
1/2 teaspoon fresh parsley, finely chopped
Squeeze lemon juice
Sea salt
Freshly ground black pepper
Parsley to garnish

SERVES
4

Method

Place the smoked mackerel fillets in a bowl and mash them with a fork. Stir in the crème fraiche, dill, parsley and mix together. Add a generous squeeze of lemon juice and season with salt and pepper. Spoon into 4 ramekin dishes, sprinkle with parsley and serve.

Vegetarian Sushi Rolls

Ingredients

1 ripe avocado, choped
150g (5 oz or 1 cup) grated carrots
150g (5oz or 1 cup) red pepper, finely chopped
150g (5oz or 1 cup) alfalfa sprouts
150g (5oz or 1 cup) brown rice
150g (5oz or 1 cup) cucumber, finely chopped
1 spring onion (scallion), finely choped
2 teaspoons fresh chives, chopped

Hummus
8 Nori sheets

SERVES 4

Method

Lay out the nori sheets (shiny side down). Spread the hummus onto the nori sheets. Across the middle of the sheet, lay a row of brown rice. Leave 1 inch of the nori sheet uncovered to seal the sushi roll. Add spring onion (scallion) carrots, cucumber, red pepper, alfalfa and avocado. Top with a sprinkling of chives. Tightly roll the nori sheet from the bottom to make a firm sushi roll. Cut into 2.5cm (1 inch) pieces and serve. As a variation on this recipe, try spreading the nori sheets with guacamole instead of hummus.

Halloumi
& Bacon Rolls

MAKES 20

Ingredients

10 rashers or slices of bacon
250g (9 oz) halloumi cheese
1 tablespoon chives, choppeds

Method

Heat the oven to 200C/400F. Cut the halloumi into 20 equal sized sticks. Sprinkle the halloumi sticks with chives. Cut the slices of bacon in half and wind it around each stick of halloumi, making a tight roll. Arrange them on a baking sheet. Place the rolls in the oven for 10-12 minutes or until the bacon is crispy.

Cajun Tuna Steaks

Ingredients

4 fresh tuna steaks
2 tablespoons Cajun seasoning
2 tablespoons olive oil
1 lemon, quartered

SERVES
4

Method

The recipe for Cajun seasoning is in the Sauces and Dips section. Generously coat the tuna with Cajun seasoning. Heat the olive oil in a large frying pan over a high heat. Place the tuna steaks in the pan and cook on one side for 3 to 4 minutes. Turn them over and cook for 3 to 4 minutes on the other side. Serve with a wedge of lemon and tabbouleh or quinoa salad.

Garlic Prawns & Mushrooms

Ingredients

2 tablespoons butter

2 tablespoons olive oil

250g (8oz) mushrooms, sliced

3 shallots, finely chopped

500g (1lb) fresh prawns, shelled

2 garlic cloves, crushed

1 tablespoon lemon juice

SERVES
4

Method

In a large frying pan, heat the oil and butter. Add the garlic, shallots and mushrooms and fry until they soften. Add the prawns, and cook until they are pink throughout. Add the lemon juice and cook for another minute. Season and serve.

Quinoa Tabbouleh

SERVES 4

Ingredients

120g (4oz or 2/3 cup) quinoa, cooked

75g (3oz or 1/2 cup) spring onions
(scallions), chopped

1 cucumber, peeled and diced

Juice of 1 lemon

1 tomato, diced

4 tablespoons fresh parsley, chopped

4 tablespoons fresh mint, chopped

1 tablespoon olive oil

Sea salt

Freshly ground black pepper

Method

Combine all the ingredients in a large bowl and mix well. Cover the tabbouleh and place it in the fridge for 20 minutes to chill or until you are ready to serve.

Tandoori Prawns

SERVES 4

Ingredients

32 large peeled, raw prawns
2 teaspoons tandoori paste
2 tablespoons natural (unflavoured) yogurt
1 lime, cut into quarters

For the raita:
3 tablespoons natural (unflavoured) yogurt
1 tablespoon fresh mint leaves, finely chopped

Method

Mix together the tandoori paste and 2 tablespoons of yogurt. Stir in the prawns, and marinate them in the fridge for at least 30 minutes. Meanwhile, mix together 3 tablespoons of yogurt and mint for the raita. Set aside. When you're ready to cook the prawns, thread 8 of them onto each skewer. Place under a hot grill (broiler) and cook for 3 minutes on each side, or until they are thoroughly cooked all the way through. Serve with wedges of lime and the raita dip on the side.

Chicken, Prosciutto & Capers

SERVES 4

Ingredients

4 medium chicken breasts
4 slices prosciutto ham
2 tablespoons capers, chopped
2 tablespoons fresh thyme, chopped
40g (1 ½ oz) butter
1 lemon, cut into slices

Method

Cover the chicken breasts with cling film (plastic wrap). Using a rolling pin beat the chicken breasts until each one is flattened. Place each chicken breast flat in an ovenproof dish and lay a slice of prosciutto on top. In a bowl, combine the butter, capers and thyme. Place a spoonful of the butter mixture on top of the prosciutto and add a slice of lemon. Transfer them to the oven and bake at 200C/400F for 25 minutes. Check that the chicken is cooked through. Serve and remember to spoon the juices on top.

Warm Chorizo & Spinach Salad

SERVES 4

Ingredients

225g (8oz) spinach leaves
3 tablespoons olive oil
25g (4oz) chorizo sausage, thinly sliced
2 tablespoons white wine vinegar
Sea salt
Freshly ground black pepper

Method

Remove any thick stalks from the spinach. Pour the olive oil into a frying pan and add the sliced chorizo. Cook for around 3 minutes. Add the spinach and white wine vinegar. Cook until the spinach has wilted. Season with salt and pepper. Serve immediately.

Cauliflower & Walnut Cheese

SERVES 4

Ingredients

1 medium cauliflower, cut into florets

50g (2oz or ½ cup) cheese, grated (shredded)

50g (2oz or ½ cup) walnuts, finely chopped (or other nuts if preferred)

1 tablespoon butter

1 clove garlic, chopped

2 tablespoons parsley

Method

Heat the butter in a frying pan. Add the walnuts and cook for one minute until lightly toasted. Add the garlic and cook for one more minute. Remove from the heat and place in a bowl to cool. Break the cauliflower into florets and steam until tender. Place in an oven proof dish. Add the cheese and parsley to the walnut mixture. Cover the steamed cauliflower with the cheese and nut mixture. Place under a hot grill (broiler) until the cheese begins to bubble. Alternatively you can place in the oven to cook the cheese and keep hot until ready to serve. You can also try this recipe with other nuts – hazelnuts work really well.

Pork, Pine Nuts & Basil

Ingredients

For the stuffing:

175g (6oz) sausage meat

2 tablespoons toasted pine nuts

2 tablespoons fresh parsley, chopped

2 tablespoons fresh basil, chopped

1 garlic clove, crushed

For the pork loin:

1kg (2lb 4oz) loin of pork

2 garlic cloves, crushed

2 tablespoons olive oil

1/2 teaspoon pepper

SERVES 6-8

Method

Lay out the pork and make a long cut lengthwise, stopping around 2 cm (1 inch) from the edge. The incision should not go right through, just create a crevice for the stuffing. Rub the 2 cloves of garlic and pepper all over the pork. In a bowl, mix together the sausage meat, pine nuts, parsley, basil and garlic. Put the sausage mixture on the inside of the pork. Pull the two sides of the pork loin together and wrap it in foil, twisting the foil at the end. Chill for 1 hour. Heat the olive oil in a pan. Unwrap the pork loin and cook in the pan for 4 minutes, turning once. Transfer to an ovenproof dish, place in the oven and cook at 180C/350F for 35 minutes. Remove, slice and serve.

Thai Chicken Burgers

Ingredients

450g (1lb) minced chicken or turkey (ground)
½ teaspoon chilli flakes
(more if you like it hot)
2 teaspoons fish sauce
2 garlic cloves, crushed
75g (3oz or ½ cup) coriander (cilantro)
2 shallots, finely chopped
2 tablespoons coconut oil
Sea salt
Freshly ground black pepper

SERVES 4

Method

Place the chicken in a large bowl and add the coriander (cilantro), fish sauce, garlic, shallots and chilli flakes. Season with salt and pepper. Mix the ingredients together well. Divide the mixture into 4 and form into burger shapes. Heat the coconut oil in a frying pan. Place the burgers in the pan and cook for around 7- 8 minutes on either side until the burgers are cooked thoroughly.

Cheesy Garlic Mushrooms

SERVES 4

Ingredients

4 large open mushrooms

2 cloves garlic, crushed

2 tablespoons fresh parsley, chopped

25g (1oz) fresh Parmesan cheese, grated

2 tablespoons olive oil

Freshly ground black pepper

Method

Remove the stalks from the mushrooms. Keep the mushroom tops and set aside. Finely chop the stalks. In a bowl, mix the garlic, parsley, chopped mushroom stalks and Parmesan cheese. Season with black pepper. Coat the mushroom tops with olive oil and place on an ovenproof dish or baking sheet. Spoon the stuffing mixture onto the mushroom tops. Cook in the oven at 190C/375F for 20 minutes. Sprinkle with fresh parsley and serve.

Cauliflower Hash Browns

Ingredients

1 fresh cauliflower, washed and grated (shredded)
4 slices bacon, finely chopped
75g (3oz) onions, finely chopped
1 teaspoon butter
Sea salt and pepper

SERVES 4-6

Method

Heat the butter in a frying pan and add the bacon and onion. Cook until the bacon starts to brown and the onion becomes soft. Add the grated cauliflower. Stir and cook until the cauliflower is tender and golden brown. Add some extra butter if you need to. Season with salt and pepper and serve.

Warm Nutty Salad

Ingredients

For the salad:

1 tablespoon olive oil

2 tomatoes, quartered and deseeded

2 spring onions (scallions), chopped

100g (3 1/2 oz or 1/2 cup) green beans

125g (4 1/2 oz or 2/3 cup) broccoli, chopped

100g (3 1/2 oz or 1/2 cup) mange tout (snow peas)

4 tablespoons macadamia nuts, chopped

For the dressing:

1 tablespoon olive oil

30ml (1fl oz or 1/8 cup) apple cider vinegar

2 tablespoons fresh thyme, finely chopped

1/2 teaspoon mustard

Freshly ground black pepper

SERVES 2

Method

For the dressing, combine the olive oil, vinegar, thyme and mustard in a bowl, season with pepper and mix well. Heat a tablespoon of olive oil in a frying pan. Add the green beans, broccoli and mange tout (snow peas). Cook for 5 minutes. Add the spring onions (scallions) and tomatoes and heat through. Add the dressing, and thoroughly coat all the vegetables. Serve into bowls while warm and sprinkle with macadamia nuts.

Smoked Haddock & Poached Eggs

SERVES 4

Ingredients

4 medium eggs

4 portions of smoked haddock

1 onion, chopped finely

400g (14oz) chopped tomatoes

2 tablespoons fresh parsley, chopped

1 tablespoon olive oil

Sea salt

Freshly ground black pepper

Method

Heat the olive oil in a frying pan and add the chopped onion. Cook for 4-5 minutes until softened. Add the tomatoes and parsley. Season with salt and pepper. Add the haddock to the tomato mixture. Cover the pan and simmer for 8-9 minutes or until the fish is cooked. Bring a saucepan of water to the boil and reduce heat until simmering gently. Stir the water with a spoon and crack one egg into the middle of the swirl. When it starts to set, push the egg towards the outside of the pan. Repeat for the other eggs. The poached eggs should be cooked for 2-3 minutes. The egg should set but be runny on the inside. Serve the fish onto plates and top each one with a poached egg. Sprinkle with a little extra parsley.

Chicken Satay Skewers

SERVES 2

Ingredients

2 skinless chicken breasts, cut into
bite-size chunks
4 tablespoons crunchy peanut butter
(sugar-free)
200ml (7fl oz or 1 cup) coconut milk
1 teaspoon soy sauce
Dash of Tabasco sauce
1 lemon, halved

Method

Preheat the oven to 200C/400F. Put the peanut butter and coconut milk into a bowl. Mix well. Add the Tabasco, soy sauce and stir. Place the chicken chunks in a bowl and pour the peanut sauce over it. Coat the chicken completely. Thread the chicken onto skewers, and set aside the remaining satay sauce. Place the chicken skewers under a hot grill (broiler) and cook for 4-5 minutes on each side, until cooked through. Place the remaining satay sauce in a small pan and add the juice from half a lemon. Heat it thoroughly. Cut the remaining lemon into 2 wedges. Serve the chicken skewers and pour the remaining satay sauce on top.

Fresh Herb & Quinoa Cakes

Ingredients

SERVES 2

100g (3 ½ oz or ¾ cup) quinoa, cooked

2 eggs

45g (2oz or ½ cup) grated Gruyere cheese

30g (1oz or ½ cup) fresh whole-wheat breadcrumbs

2 tablespoons spring onions (scallions), chopped

2 tablespoons fresh basil, chopped

2 tablespoons fresh parsley, chopped

2 teaspoons olive oil

Sea salt

Freshly ground black pepper

Method

Place the eggs in a large bowl and whisk. Add the spring onion (scallions), parsley, basil, cheese, breadcrumbs and season with salt and pepper. Mix well. Add the cooked quinoa and combine with the other ingredients. Heat the olive oil in a large frying pan. With clean hands, form 8 small patties. Place them in the frying pan and cook for about 3 minutes on each side or until golden brown.

Aubergine (Eggplant) Gratin

SERVES
4-6

Ingredients

2 ripe aubergines (eggplant)

40g (1 1/2 oz or 1/2 cup) Parmesan
cheese, grated (shredded)

2 tablespoons olive oil

Sea salt

Freshly ground black pepper

Method

Thinly slice the aubergines (eggplants) and place on a grill rack lined with foil. Brush with olive oil and grill (broil) for 15 minutes, turning once until golden on both sides. Place the aubergine slices in an oven-proof dish and cover with the grated Parmesan. Season with salt and pepper. Transfer to the oven and bake at 200C/400F for 15 minutes, or until the cheese is golden. Serve and eat immediately.

Goats Cheese & Quinoa Salad

Ingredients

- 350g (12oz) quinoa, cooked
- 225g (8oz) broccoli
- 225g (8oz) feta cheese, crumbled
- 3 tomatoes, chopped
- 3 spring onions (scallions), finely chopped
- 2 tablespoons pumpkin seeds
- 2 tablespoons fresh oregano leaves, chopped
- 2 tablespoons fresh parsley, chopped
- 3 tablespoons olive oil
- 3 tablespoons lemon juice

SERVES
4

Method

Cut the broccoli into small bite-size pieces. Add them to a steamer and cook for 5 minutes then allow it to cool. In a small frying pan, lightly toast the pumpkin seeds until they're slightly crunchy. Remove from the pan and leave to cool. Put the cooked quinoa and broccoli in a bowl and add the feta, herbs, tomato, spring onions, pumpkin seeds, olive oil and lemon juice. Toss together until everything is mixed. Season to taste and either serve straight away or store in the fridge.

Spinach & Chickpeas (Garbanzo Beans)

Ingredients

450g (1lb) fresh spinach leaves, washed

4 tablespoons olive oil

4 garlic cloves, chopped finely

400g (14oz) can of chickpeas (garbanzo beans), cooked

1 teaspoon ground cumin

1 teaspoon paprika

Juice or 1 lemon

Sea salt

Freshly ground black pepper

SERVES 4-6

Method

Heat the olive oil in a frying pan and add the chopped garlic. Cook for 1 minute to soften. Add the chickpeas (garbanzo beans), paprika, cumin, lemon juice and stir. Add the spinach, reduce the heat and simmer gently for 20 minutes, stirring occasionally. Season with salt and pepper then serve.

Butterbean & Courgette Cakes

Ingredients

1 medium courgette (zucchini)
125g (4oz or 1 cup) butter beans, rinsed
50g (2oz or 1 cup) feta cheese, crumbled
2 tablespoons fresh basil, chopped
1 spring onion (scallion), finely chopped
2 teaspoons groundnut oil or olive oil

SERVES
2

Method

Grate (shred) the courgette (zucchini) then using a tea towel and squeeze all of the liquid from it. In a large bowl, mash the butter beans with a fork then add the basil, spring onion, courgette and feta. Combine all the ingredients together well. Use your hand and mould the mixture into 4 patties. Chill them in the fridge for 10 minutes to firm up. Heat the oil in a frying pan and cook the patties on either side for around a minute. Remove them to a baking sheet and bake in the oven for 10 minutes at 220C/425F. Serve and eat immediately.

DINNER

Turkey & Sweet Potato Pie

Ingredients

2 sweet potatoes, peeled and sliced
1 tablespoon butter
600g (1lb 5oz) turkey mince (ground turkey)
2 teaspoons olive oil
1 onion, chopped finely
2 carrots, chopped
1 teaspoon dried thyme
450ml (1 pint) chicken stock (broth)
150g (5oz) broccoli
1 garlic clove, crushed
1 teaspoon plain flour (all purpose flour)
Sea salt and pepper

SERVES 4

Method

Heat the olive oil in a pan and fry the turkey mince for 7 minutes. Transfer it to a bowl. Add the broccoli, onion and carrots to the pan and fry until they soften. Add the thyme and garlic. Cook for 1 minute. Sprinkle in the flour and stir well then add the chicken stock. Add the turkey to the pan, reduce the heat and simmer for 10 minutes. Transfer the ingredients to an ovenproof casserole dish. Boil the sweet potatoes for 10-15 minutes, drain and mash them with butter and season with salt and pepper. Spread it over the turkey mixture. Bake in the oven at 200C/400F for 35-40 minutes until hot.

Chicken Chilli

Ingredients

4 chicken breasts, sliced
2 x 400g (2 x 14oz) cans of chopped tomatoes
475ml (1 pint) chicken stock
250g (9 oz) chorizo sausage, finely chopped
1 red pepper, finely chopped
400g (14oz) can of kidney beans
1 onion, finely chopped
2 garlic cloves, crushed
2 teaspoons chilli powder (more if you like it hot)
2 teaspoons ground cumin
1 teaspoon paprika
1 tablespoon olive oil

SERVES
4-6

Method

Warm the oil in a frying pan, add the garlic and onion and cook until soft. Add the chilli, cumin, paprika and stir. Pour in the tomatoes. Add the stock (broth) and bring to the boil. Add the red pepper, chorizo and sliced chicken breasts. Stir and cover. Reduce the heat and simmer for around 15 minutes. Add the kidney beans and simmer for 20 minutes. Serve with brown rice or serve the chilli in a bowl and spoon it into lettuce leaves, topped with guacamole and cheese. Strong leaf lettuce like romaine and iceberg work best. Without the rice, this low carbohydrate option will still leave you feeling satisfied.

Sausage & Squash Mash

SERVES 4

Ingredients

1 butternut squash, peeled and diced

2 sweet potatoes, peeled and diced

8 top-quality sausages

2 apples, cored, peeled and cut into wedges

1/4 teaspoon ground cinnamon

2 teaspoons butter

2 tablespoons wholegrain mustard

1/2 teaspoon ground nutmeg

Method

Sprinkle the apple wedges with cinnamon and add them to the baking tray. Cover the sausages with mustard and place them on the baking tray also. Transfer to the oven and cook for 20-25 minutes on 200C/400F, until golden brown. In the meantime, add the squash and sweet potatoes to a saucepan of boiling water. Bring to the boil then reduce the heat. Simmer for around 15 minutes, or until tender. Drain the squash and sweet potato, add the butter and ground nutmeg then mash them until no lumps remain. Serve dollops of the squash mash onto plates and serve with the sausages, apple and cooking juices.

Pork & Pepper Sauce

Ingredients

1 teaspoon coarsely ground black pepper
½ teaspoon sea salt
4 boneless pork chops
100g (3 ½ oz or ⅔ cup) mushrooms
2 tablespoons olive oil
1 medium shallot, finely chopped
180ml (6fl oz or ¾ cup) crème fraiche

**SERVES
4**

Method

Sprinkle the pork chops with ¼ teaspoon black pepper and ¼ teaspoon salt and pat onto both sides of each pork chop. Heat the oil in a frying pan and add the chops. Reduce the heat and fry for 3 or 4 minutes per side, or until cooked through. Transfer the chops to a plate and cover with foil to keep them warm. Place the mushrooms and shallot in the frying pan. Cook for 4 minutes until they soften. Add the crème fraiche and the remaining ¼ teaspoon salt and ¾ teaspoon black pepper and stir until the sauce is thoroughly heated. Serve the pork chops with the mushrooms and sauce. Celeriac mash is a brilliant accompaniment to this dish.

Vegetarian Nut Loaf

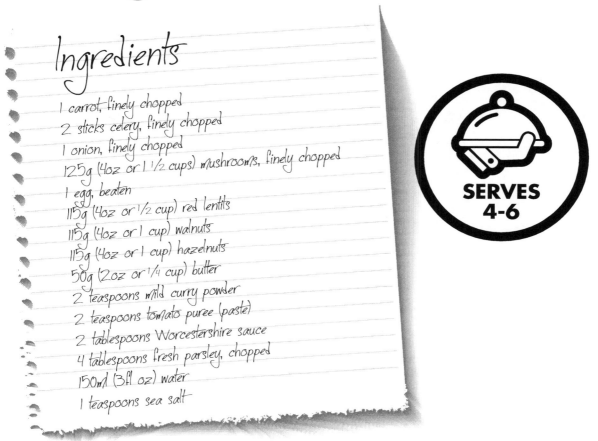

Ingredients

1 carrot, finely chopped
2 sticks celery, finely chopped
1 onion, finely chopped
125g (4oz or 1 1/2 cups) mushrooms, finely chopped
1 egg, beaten
115g (4oz or 1/2 cup) red lentils
115g (4oz or 1 cup) walnuts
115g (4oz or 1 cup) hazelnuts
50g (2oz or 1/4 cup) butter
2 teaspoons mild curry powder
2 teaspoons tomato puree (paste)
2 tablespoons Worcestershire sauce
4 tablespoons fresh parsley, chopped
150ml (3fl oz) water
1 teaspoons sea salt

SERVES 4-6

Method

Steep the lentils in cold water for 1 hour. Heat the butter in a pan and add the carrot, celery, onion, mushrooms and curry powder. Stir and cook for 5 minutes. Blitz the nuts in a food processor, and set aside. Drain the lentils, place them in a bowl and add the nuts. Stir in the vegetables, tomato paste, Worcestershire sauce, egg, parsley, water and salt. Grease and line a large loaf tin with greaseproof paper. Put the mixture into the tin and smooth out. Cover with foil. Bake in the oven at 190C/375F for 60-90 minutes. Let it stand for 10 minutes and turn onto a serving plate.

Bacon & Sweet Potato Hash

SERVES
4

Ingredients

750g (1lb 11oz) sweet potato, peeled and
cut into small cubes
150g (5oz) broccoli, broken into small
florets
6 slices of bacon, roughly chopped
1 small onion, thinly sliced
1 tablespoon olive oil
Sea salt
Freshly ground black pepper

Method

Steam the sweet potato for 10 minutes. Add the broccoli to the steamer and cook for
another 4 minutes. Heat the olive oil in a frying pan. Add the bacon and onion. Fry until
the bacon is cooked. Add the sweet potato and broccoli to the pan and stir. Cook for
around 10 minutes, stirring to dislodge the crispy bottom.

Hot Barbecued Chicken Wings

Ingredients

20 chicken wings

Barbeque sauce

1/2 teaspoon chilli powder

1 teaspoon onion powder

1 teaspoon ground cumin

1 teaspoon cayenne pepper (less if you like it milder)

1 teaspoon garlic salt

2 teaspoons paprika

2 1/2 tablespoons apple cider vinegar

1 teaspoon black pepper

1 teaspoon mustard

1/2 teaspoon stevia (optional)

3 tablespoons olive oil

MAKES 20

Method

In a bowl, mix together all the barbeque sauce ingredients and stir really well. Preheat the oven to 200C/400F. Dip the chicken wings in the sauce and place them on a large baking sheet. Transfer them to the oven and roast for 30 minutes, until the chicken wings are cooked through and well browned. Transfer to a serving plate and enjoy.

Mussels, Garlic & Herbs

Ingredients

900g (2lb) fresh mussels
1 wedge of lemon
3 tablespoons olive oil
2 shallots, finely chopped
2 clove garlic, finely chopped
2 tablespoons fresh parsley, chopped
1/2 teaspoon paprika
1/2 teaspoon chilli flakes

SERVES 4

Method

Wash the mussels and remove the beard. Discard any mussels that don't close when tapped with a knife. Place the mussels in a pan with 250ml (1 cup) water and the wedge of lemon. Cover and bring to the boil over a high heat for around 5-6 minutes. Remove from heat. Check for any mussels that haven't opened and discard them. Pull apart the cooked mussels and remove the shells. In a frying pan, heat the olive oil. Add the mussels and cook for around a minute. Remove from the pan and set aside. Add the garlic and shallots to the pan and cook on a low heat for 5 minutes. Remove the pan from the heat, stir in the parsley, paprika and chilli. Stir in the cooked mussels and heat through before serving.

Celeriac Mash

Ingredients
- 1 celeriac
- 25g (1oz) butter
- Salt & pepper

SERVES
4

Method

Peel the celeriac and chop it into chunks. Put it in a saucepan of cold water. Bring to the boil, reduce the heat and simmer for 20 minutes. Drain the celeriac, add the butter and mash. Season and serve with rich meat dishes.

Sweet Potato Mash

Ingredients

700g (1lb 9 oz) sweet potato, peeled and chopped
1/2 teaspoon nutmeg

1/2 teaspoon cinnamon
1 teaspoon ground ginger,
2 teaspoons butter

SERVES
4-6

Method

Place the sweet potatoes in a saucepan, bring to the boil and simmer for 10-12 minutes, until soft. Drain the sweet potatoes but leave them in the saucepan. Add the ginger, nutmeg, cinnamon and butter to the sweet potatoes and mash them until they become smooth. Season and serve.

Chicken & Vegetable Casserole

Ingredients

4 large chicken leg quarters
600ml (1 pint) chicken or vegetable stock
3 stalks of celery
2 carrots
1 courgette (zucchini)
1 onion
2 sage leaves
1 bay leaf
1 teaspoon thyme
2 sprigs rosemary
Freshly ground black pepper

SERVES 4

Method

Preheat the oven to 170C/325F. Season the chicken pieces with black pepper and place in an oven-proof casserole dish. Roughly chop the carrots, celery, courgette (zucchini) and onion and add to the casserole dish. Now add the stock to the chicken and chopped vegetables. Add the sage, thyme, rosemary and bay leaf. Cover and place in the oven for 1 hour. Check to make sure the chicken is cooked thoroughly. Remove the rosemary stalks and bay leaf before serving.

Lamb Kebabs & Cucumber Raita

Ingredients

450g (1lb) boneless lamb
150g (5oz) natural yogurt (unflavoured)
1 teaspoon ground cumin
1 teaspoon ground coriander (cilantro)
Juice of 1/2 a lemon
Cucumber Raita
2 tablespoons fresh coriander, chopped
1/2 cucumber, seeds removed and diced finely
250g (9 oz) natural yogurt (unflavoured)

SERVES 4

Method

Chop the lamb into bite-size chunks. In a bowl, combine the 150g (5oz) yogurt, cumin, coriander (cilantro) and lemon juice. Add the lamb to the marinade, cover and place in the fridge for one hour. (It's even better if you can leave it overnight). Meanwhile make the raita by combining the 250g (9oz) yogurt, chopped cucumber and coriander. Chill in the fridge. Once the lamb is marinated, thread the lamb chunks onto skewers. Place under a hot grill (broiler) for 5 minutes on either side. Serve alongside the cucumber.

Salmon Burgers

Ingredients

600g (1 ½ lb) boneless salmon fillet
2 tablespoons fresh dill
2 tablespoons fresh parsley
1 garlic clove
1 egg
1 spring onion

SERVES 4-6

Method

Place the salmon in a food processor with the spring onion, dill, parsley and garlic. Blend until smooth. Place the mixture in a medium bowl and combine with the egg. Using your hands, shape the mixture into patties. Place under a grill for 15 minutes, turning once halfway through.

Bolognese Stuffed Aubergines (Eggplants)

Ingredients

- 750g (1lb 11oz) minced beef (ground beef)
- 2 x 400g tins chopped tomatoes
- 2 tablespoons olive oil
- 2 onions, finely chopped
- 4 cloves garlic chopped
- 1 carrot, finely chopped
- 1 red (Bell) pepper, finely chopped
- 2 stalks of celery, finely chopped
- 900ml (1 ½ pints or 4 cups) beef stock
- 2 tablespoons tomato paste
- 2 small aubergines (eggplants)
- 4 tablespoons fresh basil, chopped
- 100g (3 ½ oz) grated Parmesan cheese

SERVES 4-6

Method

Heat the olive oil in a large pan. Add the onion, garlic, carrot, celery and pepper. Cook for 5 minutes. Add the beef and mix well, breaking up any lumps. Cook for 5 minutes. Add the tinned tomatoes, beef stock and tomato paste. Bring to the boil then reduce heat and simmer for 40 minutes. Cut the aubergines in half and coat with a little olive oil. Bake in the oven at 200C/400F for 30 minutes. From the middle of aubergines (eggplants), scoop out the fresh, leaving a border of around 1 cm. In a bowl, combine the aubergine flesh with the Bolognese and add the basil. Spoon the mixture into the aubergine halves. Sprinkle them with parmesan cheese. Return them to the oven for 20 minutes until heated thoroughly.

Salmon & Haddock Kebabs

SERVES 4

Ingredients

350g (12oz) piece of haddock
350g (12oz) salmon steak
1 teaspoon paprika
Juice of 1 lime
Freshly ground black pepper

Method

Remove the skin and all the bones from both fish. Cut each of them into chunks and place in a bowl. Cover with the lime juice, paprika and black pepper. Once the fish is coated, slide alternating pieces of salmon and haddock onto skewers. Place the kebabs under a hot grill (broiler) and cook for 3-4 minutes on each side, until cooked through.

Turkey & Ham Wraps

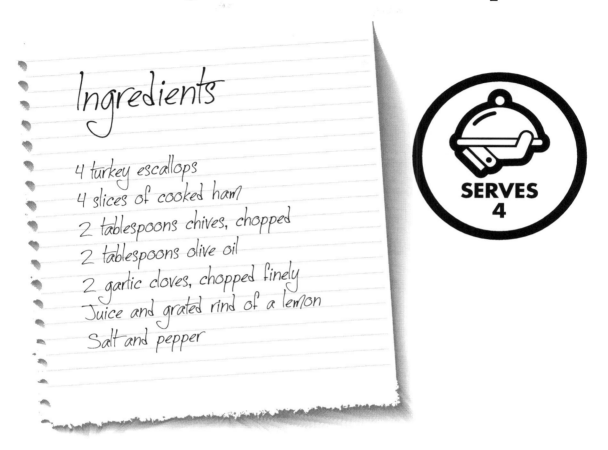

Ingredients

4 turkey escallops
4 slices of cooked ham
2 tablespoons chives, chopped
2 tablespoons olive oil
2 garlic cloves, chopped finely
Juice and grated rind of a lemon
Salt and pepper

SERVES 4

Method

Halve each turkey escalope horizontally and open it out. Season the inside of the turkey with salt and pepper, then sprinkle with garlic, lemon juice, lemon rind and chopped chives. Put the two pieces back together again. Wrap the turkey in a slice of ham and hold it together with wooden cocktail sticks. Heat the olive oil in a frying pan. Add the meat rolls and cook for 5-6 minutes until golden brown. Turn over, and coat with any remaining lemon juice. Cook for another 3-4 minutes until cooked through then serve.

Sweet & Slow Spicy Chicken

SERVES 4

Ingredients

1 onion, sliced
4 chicken leg quarters
3 garlic cloves, crushed
6cm (3 inch) chunk of fresh ginger, peeled
and sliced
2 x 400g (2 x 14oz) cans of chopped tomatoes
150g (5oz or 1 cup) pumpkin or squash,
chopped into small cubes
2 teaspoons ground cumin
2 teaspoons ground cinnamon
1 tablespoon olive oil
1/2 teaspoon sea salt
1/2 teaspoon black pepper

Method

In a large bowl combine the cumin, cinnamon, salt and pepper. Add the chicken and coat thoroughly in the spices. Heat the oil in a large pan and add the chicken, skin side down. Cook for 5 minutes until browned slightly. In a slow cooker, place the onion, garlic, and ginger. Add chicken, skin side up, then top with tomatoes, and squash. Cover and slow cook on high for around 3½ hours, or until the chicken is tender.

Scallops,
Bacon & Fennel

Ingredients

1 fennel bulb
100g (3 ½ oz or ½ cup)
mascarpone cheese
8 large scallops, shelled
75g (3oz) smoked bacon rashers

SERVES 2

Method

Slice the fennel bulbs thinly. Bring a saucepan of boiling water to the boil, add the fennel and cook for 3 minutes until tender. Drain and set aside. Preheat the grill (broiler). Put the fennel in a heat-proof dish. Place small dollops of mascarpone on the fennel and grill until the cheese has melted and is beginning to brown. Grill the bacon until crispy. Crumble it and set aside, keeping it warm. Fry the scallops for 1-2 minutes on each side, until cooked. Serve the fennel and mascarpone onto plates, sprinkle on the crumbled bacon and keep a little back to garnish with. Place the scallops on top and top with a sprinkling of bacon. Eat immediately.

Rosemary & Garlic Roast Chicken

SERVES 4-6

Ingredients

1 large whole chicken
1 tablespoon olive oil
2 tablespoons fresh rosemary, finely chopped
6 cloves of garlic, finely chopped
1 teaspoon sea salt
Freshly ground black pepper

Method

Preheat your oven to 180C/350F. Place the garlic, rosemary and salt in a small bowl and combine. Make an opening at the neck of the chicken and tuck the rosemary and garlic mixture under the skin. Loosen the skin around the drumsticks and press it in. Sprinkle with pepper. Place the chicken in an ovenproof dish, with a tablespoon of olive oil and cook for around 1½-1¾ hours basting with the cooking juices. When the juices run clear, remove from the oven and allow it to stand for a few minutes before serving.

Lemon
& Thyme Chicken

**SERVES
6**

Ingredients

9 00g (2lb) chicken thighs
10 stems of fresh thyme
250ml (8fl oz or 1 cup)
vegetable stock (broth)
4 lemons
Salt and pepper

Method

Preheat the oven to 180C/350F. Take the leaves from 5 of the stems of thyme, make small incisions and insert them between the chicken skin and the meat. Place in an oven-proof dish and season with salt and pepper. Pour in the stock (broth). Quarter the lemons and add them to the dish. Add the remaining thyme sprigs. Place the chicken in the oven and roast for 30 – 40 minutes, or until the chicken is cooked thoroughly.

Pesto & Mozzarella Chicken

Ingredients

300g (11oz) mozzarella cheese
4 chicken breasts
1 tablespoon pitted green olives
1 tablespoon pitted black olives
4 tablespoons basil pesto
2 tomatoes
Fresh basil leaves
5 tablespoons olive oil
Freshly ground black pepper

SERVES 4

Method

Slice the mozzarella, tomatoes and olives then leave aside. Heat 1 tablespoon of olive oil in a frying pan and fry the chicken for 1 minute on either side. Put the remaining oil in an oven-proof dish and add the chicken breasts. Spread a teaspoon of basil pesto onto each chicken breast. Sprinkle them with olives, add the sliced tomatoes and top with mozzarella. Season with pepper and bake at 200C/400F for 20-25 minutes. Serve and garnish with pesto and a few basil leaves.

Zesty Herby Quinoa Salad

Ingredients

225g (8oz) quinoa, cooked

6 spring onions, (scallions), finely chopped

6 cherry tomatoes, quartered

1/2 a cucumber, diced

2 tablespoons fresh basil, finely chopped

2 tablespoons fresh coriander, (cilantro), finely chopped

2 tablespoons fresh parsley, finely chopped

6 pitted olives, finely chopped

2 cloves garlic, crushed

60ml (2fl oz or 1/4 cup) olive oil

Juice of 2 large lemons

1/4 teaspoon sea salt

1/4 teaspoon freshly ground black pepper

SERVES 2

Method

In a large bowl, mix together the garlic, olive oil, lemon juice, salt, and pepper. Add the quinoa, spring onions, tomatoes, cucumber, olives, and herbs. Toss all the ingredients in the dressing until it's thoroughly coated. Chill in the fridge for 1 hour before serving.

Chilli Beef & Baby Corn

Ingredients

2 tablespoons groundnut oil

300g (11oz) beef strips, or steak cut into thin strips

200g (7oz) baby corn

200g (7oz) asparagus, chopped

1 small onion, sliced

2 red chillies, deseeded and finely sliced

Juice of 1/2 a lime

1 clove garlic, crushed

2 tablespoons soy sauce

SERVES 2

Method

Heat the oil in a wok or large frying pan. Add the garlic and chilli. Cook for 30 seconds. Add the baby corn, onion and asparagus and cook for 3 minutes. Add the beef and fry for 2-3 minutes or until the meat is lightly browned. Add the lime juice and soy sauce. Cook until heated through and serve with rice and salad. The beauty of baby corn is that it is low in carbohydrate unlike sweetcorn kernels.

Winter Warming Lamb

Ingredients

- 675g (1 1/2 lb) boneless lamb, cut into cubes
- 2 tablespoons coconut oil
- 1 large onion, chopped
- 1 carrot, chopped
- 2 stalks celery
- 1 parsnip, chopped
- 2 cloves garlic, chopped
- 1 tablespoon fresh ginger, chopped finely
- 1 teaspoon ground coriander (cilantro)
- 1 teaspoon ground cinnamon
- 1/4 teaspoon chilli flakes (or more if required)
- 1/4 teaspoon ground cloves
- 3 tomatoes, chopped
- 120 ml (4fl oz or 1/2 cup) chicken or vegetable stock (broth)
- 4 tablespoons fresh coriander (cilantro)

SERVES 4-6

Method

In a large saucepan, heat the coconut oil. Add the lamb in batches, browning on all sides. Reduce the heat and add in the onion, carrot, parsnip, garlic, cinnamon, cloves, ginger, chilli and coriander (cilantro). Cook for 5 minutes. Add the lamb, tomatoes and stock and bring to boil. Reduce the heat and simmer for 45 minutes. Sprinkle with a little fresh coriander and serve.

Prawns & Lemon Quinoa

Ingredients

200g (7oz or 2 cups) quinoa, cooked
450g (1lb) raw prawns, shelled
400g (14oz) butter beans, rinsed and drained
2 tablespoons capers
½ teaspoon paprika
2 tablespoons butter
Juice of 1 lemon
3 tablespoons olive oil
2 tablespoon fresh parsley, chopped

SERVES
4

Method

In a hot pan, heat 2 tablespoons of the oil. Add the prawns and paprika and fry for 3-4 minutes until cooked through. Transfer to a plate and set aside. Put the beans, capers, butter and lemon juice in the pan and cook for 2 minutes. Add to the pan the parsley and the remaining tablespoon of olive oil and stir. Finally, add the quinoa and combine. Season and serve the quinoa topped with the paprika prawns.

Thai Red Curry Vegetables

Ingredients

SERVES 4-6

- 2 tablespoons coconut oil
- 1 red pepper (Bell pepper), chopped
- 1 green pepper (Bell pepper), chopped
- 1 onion, chopped
- 1 bunch spring onions (scallions), chopped
- 100g broccoli, broken into small florets
- 1 medium carrot, chopped
- 3 teaspoons Thai red curry paste
- 400ml (14fl oz) coconut milk
- 1 tablespoon fresh coriander (cilantro), chopped
- 50g (2oz) chopped peanuts, to garnish

Method

Heat the coconut oil in a large pan. Add the onion, carrots and broccoli and fry for 5 minutes. Add the remaining vegetables and cook for a further 3 minutes. Add the curry paste and coconut milk. Cover and simmer for 10 minutes until the vegetables are tender but firm. Add the chopped coriander (cilantro) and stir. Transfer to serving bowls and sprinkle with chopped peanuts and a little coriander.

Chicken, Avocado & Black Eyed Peas

SERVES 2

Ingredients

200g (7oz or 1 cup) black eyed peas
2 cooked chicken breasts, sliced
1/2 cucumber, chopped
1 avocado, flesh scooped out
2 tomatoes, chopped
6 Romaine lettuce leaves
1/2 teaspoon Tabasco sauce
Juice of 1/2 lemon
2 teaspoons olive oil

Method

Rinse and drain the black-eyed peas then place them in a bowl. Add the chicken slices, tomato and cucumber to the bowl. Put the avocado, lemon juice, Tabasco, and olive oil in a food processor and blitz until smooth. Combine the avocado mixture with the chicken and black eyed peas. Scoop the chicken and avocado mixture into the lettuce leaves, ready to eat.

Pulled Beef

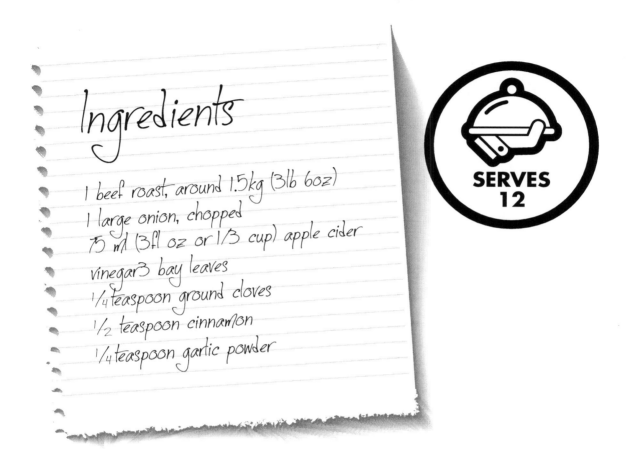

Ingredients

1 beef roast, around 1.5kg (3lb 6oz)
1 large onion, chopped
75 ml (3fl oz or 1/3 cup) apple cider vinegar
3 bay leaves
1/4 teaspoon ground cloves
1/2 teaspoon cinnamon
1/4 teaspoon garlic powder

SERVES 12

Method

This dish is best prepared the evening before you need it. Place the beef and onion in a slow cooker. Mix together the vinegar, bay leaves, ground cloves, cinnamon and garlic powder then pour over the beef. Put the lid on the slow cooker and cook on low for 10-12 hours, or until the meat is very tender. Remove and discard the bay leaves. Remove the meat and shred it with a fork and it's ready to eat.

Kidney Bean & Vegetable Chilli

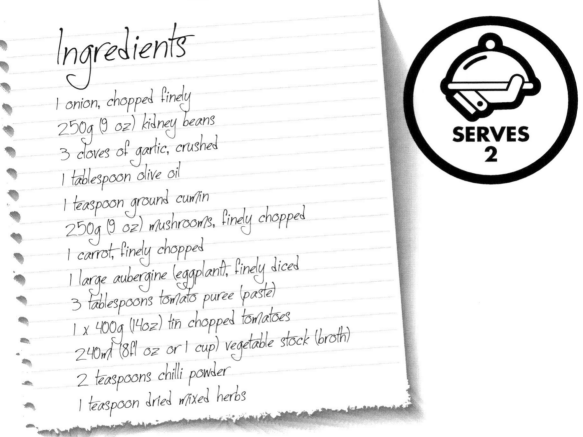

Ingredients

1 onion, chopped finely
250g (9 oz) kidney beans
3 cloves of garlic, crushed
1 tablespoon olive oil
1 teaspoon ground cumin
250g (9 oz) mushrooms, finely chopped
1 carrot, finely chopped
1 large aubergine (eggplant), finely diced
3 tablespoons tomato puree (paste)
1 x 400g (14oz) tin chopped tomatoes
240ml (8fl oz or 1 cup) vegetable stock (broth)
2 teaspoons chilli powder
1 teaspoon dried mixed herbs

SERVES 2

Method

In a large saucepan, heat the olive oil. Add the onion and garlic and soften slightly. Add the mushrooms, carrot, tinned tomatoes, aubergine (eggplant), tomato paste, vegetable stock (broth), chilli, cumin and mixed herbs. Bring to the boil then simmer for 30 minutes, stirring occasionally. Add the kidney beans and cook for another 10 minutes. Serve with brown rice, or go carb free and spoon the chilli into romaine or iceberg lettuce leaves. Top it with guacamole and grated cheese – it is filling and you won't miss the rice!

Parmesan Chicken Drumsticks

SERVES 4

Ingredients

9 0g (3 ½ oz or 1 cup) Parmesan cheese, grated

50g (2oz) butter

1 teaspoon ground oregano

2 teaspoons paprika

2 teaspoons dried parsley

½ teaspoon black pepper

12 chicken drumsticks

Method

Place the Parmesan, oregano, paprika, parsley and pepper in a bowl and stir, mixing thoroughly. Coat each chicken drumstick in butter. Roll the drumstick in the seasoned Parmesan mixture and place it on the baking tray. Bake in the oven at 180C/350F for 35 minutes, until slightly golden.

Spinach & Coconut Dahl

Ingredients

125g (4oz) spinach
450g (1lb) lentils
400ml (14fl oz) coconut milk
1 large onion, chopped
2cm (1in) chunk of ginger, peeled and finely chopped
1 tomato, chopped
1 teaspoon chilli powder (or 1 chilli, deseeded & chopped)
3 cardamom pods
3 garlic cloves, chopped
1 ½ teaspoons ground cumin
1 ½ teaspoon ground coriander (cilantro)
½ teaspoon turmeric
2 tablespoons fresh coriander (cilantro), chopped
1 bay leaf
1 tablespoon coconut oil

SERVES 4

Method

Heat the coconut oil in a large saucepan. Add the onion, tomato, cumin, ginger, ground coriander, chilli, turmeric, garlic and cardamom seeds and cook for about 10 minutes or until the onion is soft. Add the coconut milk, bay leaf and lentils. Cook for 20 minutes. Add the spinach and stir. Cook for another 3 minutes. Just before serving, add the fresh coriander and stir. Remove the bay leaf. Serve with a salad or brown rice.

Sausage & Tomato Casserole

Ingredients

SERVES 6

1 tablespoon olive oil
12 top-quality sausages
50g (2oz) pancetta, finely chopped
2 onions, roughly chopped
2 garlic cloves, crushed
1 red pepper (Bell pepper), chopped
2 x 400g tins of chopped tomatoes
Sea salt
Freshly ground black pepper

Method

Heat the oil in a pan, add the sausages and pancetta and fry for 10 minutes until the sausages are nicely golden and the pancetta is crispy. Remove and set aside. Remove the excess fat. Put the onions and garlic in the pan and cook for 4 minutes then add the chopped red pepper and fry for another 2 minutes. Add the sausages and pancetta to the pan and stir in the chopped tomatoes. Cover the pan and cook on a medium heat for 20 minutes. Season with salt and pepper and serve.

Braised Beef & Mushrooms

Ingredients

1.35kg (3lb) braising steak (chuck steak), thickly sliced

2 carrots, chopped

250g (9 oz) mushrooms

2 onions, thinly sliced

3 tablespoons olive oil

1 tablespoon thyme, fresh or dried

1 tablespoon plain (all purpose) flour

Sea salt

Freshly ground black pepper

SERVES 8

Method

Season the beef on both sides with salt and pepper. Heat 2 tablespoons of olive oil in a pan, then add the meat and brown it for 4 minutes. Remove the meat from the pan and set aside. Add to the pan 1 tablespoon of olive oil then add the onions and fry until softened. Return the meat to the pan, sprinkle in the flour and cook for 1 min. Place the onions and meat in an oven-proof casserole dish. Add the mushrooms, carrots and thyme. Season and cover. Cook in the oven at 150C/300F for 1½-2 hours until the meat is tender. Serve it with butternut squash or celeriac mash.

DESSERTS, SWEET TREATS & SNACKS

Sweet Potato Chips

Ingredients

2 large sweet potatoes, peeled
2 tablespoons coconut oil
2 teaspoons cinnamon

SERVES
2-4

Method

Cut the sweet potatoes into chips (fries). Transfer to a bowl of water and leave them to stand for 40 minutes. Pat them dry with a clean tea towel. If the coconut oil is solid, melt it and put it in a large bowl along with the cinnamon. Add the sweet potatoes and toss to completely coat them.

Grease a baking sheet and lay the chips out. Transfer to the oven and bake at 200C/400F for 15 minutes, turn the chips over and bake for another 15 minutes. You can adapt this recipe by adding curry powder or paprika as a savoury option.

Balti Mixed Nuts

Ingredients

2 tablespoons coconut oil
80g (3oz or ½ cup) cashew nuts
80g (3oz or ½ cup) Brazil nuts
80g (3oz or ½ cup) walnuts
½ teaspoon curry powder
½ teaspoon garlic powder
½ teaspoon paprika

SERVES
6-8

Method

Heat the coconut oil in a large frying pan. Add all of the nuts, the curry powder, garlic and paprika to the hot pan. Stir and cook for around 7-8 minutes. Store or serve as a party nibble or snack. Try substituting the spices for cinnamon, for a sweeter variation.

Courgette Chips (Zucchini)

Ingredients

1 large courgette (zucchini)
1 teaspoon olive oil
Sea salt

(paprika, cayenne pepper or garlic powder can be used)

SERVES
2

Method

Slice the courgette (zucchini) into thin circles, around the thickness of a coin. Place them in a bowl, add a teaspoon of olive oil and seasoning. Toss to lightly coat them. Line a baking sheet with foil, and lay out the slices onto the sheet. Preheat the oven to 220C/425F and bake the chips 30 minutes, turning once. Remove when crispy and golden. Serve and eat immediately.

Baked Kale Chips

Ingredients

1 bag of fresh kale
1 tablespoon olive oil
Sea salt

SERVES
4

Method

Remove the tough stalks from the kale and cut the leaves into bite-size squares of around 3cm. Place the olive oil and salt in a bowl and toss the kale to coat it. Place it on a baking tray. Transfer the kale to the oven and bake at 170C/325F for 6-10 minutes or until the kale is crispy.

Baked Radish Chips

Ingredients

20 radishes, cleaned and ends trimmed
1 tablespoon olive oil
1/4 teaspoon garlic powder
1/4 teaspoon paprika
1/4 teaspoon of salt

SERVES 6-8

Method

Cut the radishes ¼ inch thick. Place them in a bowl with the olive oil garlic powder, paprika and salt. Coat the radishes thoroughly. Line a baking sheet with greaseproof paper and lay out the radishes. Transfer them to the oven and bake them at 220C/450F for 20 minutes. Turn them over and cook for another 20 minutes. When they are crispy and have shrunk in size they are done. Serve and eat immediately.

Almond & Cherry 'Cheesecake'

SERVES 2

Ingredients

300g (12oz) cherries, stones removed

50g (2oz) flaked almonds

75g (3oz) ground almonds

200g (8oz) ricotta cheese

1/4 teaspoon cinnamon

Method

Heat the cherries in a saucepan for around 8 minutes, until they are soft and warmed through then add the cinnamon. Sprinkle the ground almonds onto the bottom of two serving bowls. Spoon the ricotta cheese on top. Pour the warm cherries over the ricotta. Sprinkle with flaked almonds. Eat immediately.

Star Anise &
Cinnamon Spiced Pears

**SERVES
4**

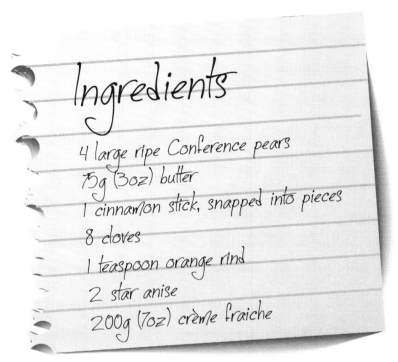

Ingredients

4 large ripe Conference pears

75g (3oz) butter

1 cinnamon stick, snapped into pieces

8 cloves

1 teaspoon orange rind

2 star anise

200g (7oz) crème fraiche

Method

Peel the pears and trim the bottom slightly to allow it to stand up. Heat the butter in a frying pan, add the cinnamon, cloves and star anise. Once the butter is warm, add the pears. Gently cook for 10-15 minutes, basting the pears with the butter and spice. In a bowl, combine the crème fraiche with the orange rind then set aside. When the pears are soft, transfer them to serving bowls and add a side dollop of the crème fraiche.

Choc & Nut Brittle

Ingredients

150g Brazil nuts, chopped
75g (3oz) coconut oil
75g (3oz) butter
2 tablespoons 100% cocoa powder
2 teaspoons stevia powder

MAKES 24

Method

Melt the butter and coconut oil in a saucepan. Stir in the cocoa powder and stevia and mix until smooth. Place half of the chopped Brazil nuts in the bottom of a small dish or small loaf tin. Pour on half the chocolate mixture. Sprinkle on the remaining chopped nuts and add the remaining chocolate. Chill for at least an hour until the chocolate is hard. Using a knife, cut it into 24 small pieces, or break it into large rough chunks and serve. The coconut oil in the chocolate will melt in a warm room, so it needs to be kept chilled until ready to eat. As a variation, try adding chopped banana with the Brazil nuts before covering with chocolate. It's so delicious.

Peanut Butter Chocolates

Ingredients

75g (3oz) coconut oil
75g (3oz) butter
2 tablespoons 100% cocoa powder
2 teaspoons stevia powder
100g (3 ½ oz) crunchy peanut butter
(or almond, cashew or pistachio butter)

MAKES
20

Method

Put the coconut oil, butter, cocoa powder and stevia powder into a saucepan and heat until the butter and coconut oil have melted. Set out small paper cake cases, petit four size works best. Spoon half the chocolate mixture into the bottom of the paper cases. Only fill each case half way up. Allow to cool slightly. Add approximately 1 teaspoon of peanut butter onto the chocolate in the cases. You may need to re-heat the chocolate if it's beginning to set. Spoon the remaining chocolate into the cases to completely cover the peanut butter. Chill in the fridge for 1 hour.

Coconut Finger Bars

Ingredients

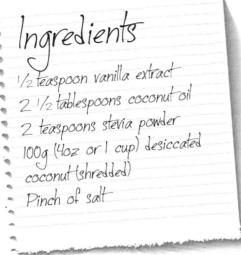

- ½ teaspoon vanilla extract
- 2 ½ tablespoons coconut oil
- 2 teaspoons stevia powder
- 100g (4oz or 1 cup) desiccated coconut (shredded)
- Pinch of salt

SERVES 8

Method

Place all of the ingredients in a food processor and blitz until smooth. Scrape out the coconut mixture and put in the bottom of a loaf tin or small rectangular container. Spread and smooth the mixture. Chill in the fridge for one hour. Cut into 8 slices and keep chilled until you're ready to eat them.

Banana Milk Shake

Ingredients

- 200ml (7fl oz or 1 cup) almond milk
- 1 tablespoon peanut butter
- ½ banana
- ½ tsp cinnamon

SERVES 1

Method

Place all the ingredients into a blender and blitz until smooth.

Almond & Cardamom Bananas

SERVES 4

Ingredients

4 tablespoons plain (unflavoured) yogurt

1 vanilla pod

5 tablespoons coconut oil

4 bananas, peeled and halved lengthways

3 cardamom pods, seeds removed and crushed

4 tablespoons flaked almonds

Zest and juice of 1 lime

Method

Place the yogurt in a bowl, scrape out the vanilla seeds and stir them in. Set aside. Heat 1 tablespoon of coconut oil in a frying pan. Add the bananas and cook for about 2 minutes on each side until golden. Put the bananas into serving dishes. Using the same pan, heat 4 tablespoons of coconut oil. Add the crushed cardamom seeds, and flaked almonds and heat for around a minute. Add in the lime juice and zest. Stir until it begins to bubble. Pour the sauce over the bananas. Spoon the yogurt alongside the bananas. Serve and eat straight away.

Raspberry Chocolate Frozen Yogurt

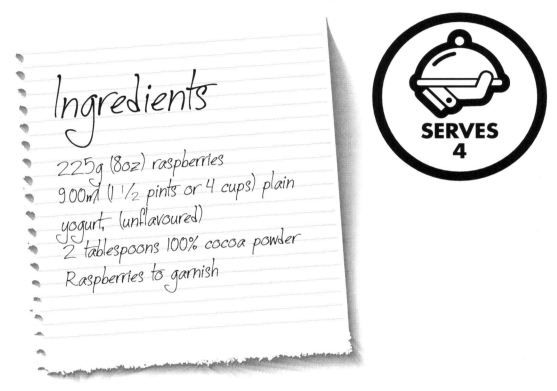

SERVES 4

Ingredients

225g (8oz) raspberries
900ml (1 ½ pints or 4 cups) plain yogurt, (unflavoured)
2 tablespoons 100% cocoa powder
Raspberries to garnish

Method

Place the raspberries in a bowl and mash with a fork. Add ½ the yogurt and stir until combined. In another bowl, combine the remaining yogurt and cocoa powder. Line a small loaf tin with grease-proof paper or plastic wrap. Spread ½ the raspberry yogurt mixture into the prepared tin and smooth it. Top it with the chocolate yogurt mixture then add the remaining raspberry mixture. Freeze for at least 3 hours, or until firm. Place a serving plate over the tin and gently tip out the frozen dessert. Remove the wrap. Garnish with a few fresh raspberries, slice and serve.

Yogurt Toppers

Yogurt is so versatile and can be eaten as a snack, for breakfast or after a meal. You can liven up your plain yogurt to make it more of a treat. Here are a few suggestions..

COCONUT & BRAZIL NUT

Chop a tablespoon of toasted coconut flakes and a tablespoon of chopped Brazil. Sprinkle them onto your bowl of yogurt for extra flavour and crunch.

CHOCOLATE, BANANA & PECAN NUTS

Cut the banana into diagonal slices, roughly chop the pecan nuts and add both to your yogurt. Sprinkle with cocoa powder and enjoy.

RASPBERRY & FLAKED ALMOND

Place a handful of raspberries in a pan, add a pinch of cinnamon and add a squeeze of lemon juice. Pour the warm raspberries over your bowl of yogurt and top it if off with flaked almonds.

SAUCES
AND DIPS

Guacamole

Ingredients
- 2 ripe avocados
- 1 clove garlic
- 1 red chilli pepper, finely chopped
- Juice of 1 lime
- 2 tablespoons fresh coriander leaves (cilantro), chopped

Method
Remove the stone from the avocado and scoop out the flesh. Combine all the ingredients in a bowl and mash together until smooth. Garnish with fresh coriander.

Hummus

Ingredients
- 240g (8oz) can of chickpeas, drained
- 2 cloves garlic
- 1 teaspoon sea salt
- Juice of 1 lemon
- 1 tablespoon olive oil

Method
Place all the ingredients in a blender until it is combined. Transfer the hummus into a bowl and it's ready to serve as a dip for crudities.

Barbecue Sauce

Ingredients

½ teaspoon cayenne pepper
1 teaspoon garlic salt
2 teaspoons paprika
1 teaspoon cinnamon
2 tablespoons apple cider vinegar

1 teaspoon pepper
1 teaspoon mustard
1 teaspoon cumin
½ teaspoon stevia (optional)
2 tablespoons olive oil

Method

Place all of the ingredients in a small bowl and stir well. Store or use the sauce straight away. It works great with ribs, pork, chicken wings, or beef.

Basil Pesto

Ingredients

4 tablespoons pine nuts
6 tablespoons chopped basil leaves
80g (3 ½ oz) Parmesan cheese, finely grated
1 clove of garlic
2 tablespoons olive oil

Method

Put all of the ingredients into a food processor or blend until you have a smooth paste.

118

Coriander Pesto (Cilantro)

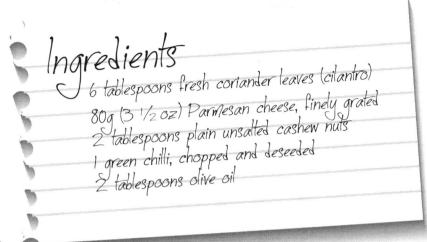

Ingredients

- 6 tablespoons fresh coriander leaves (cilantro)
- 80g (3 ½ oz) Parmesan cheese, finely grated
- 2 tablespoons plain unsalted cashew nuts
- 1 green chilli, chopped and deseeded
- 2 tablespoons olive oil

Method

Place all the ingredients in a food processor and blitz until it becomes a smooth paste.

Sugar-Free Cajun Seasoning

Ingredients

- 2½ tablespoons paprika
- 2 tablespoons sea salt
- 2 tablespoons garlic powder
- 1 tablespoon onion powder
- 1 tablespoon cayenne pepper
- 1 tablespoon dried oregano
- 1 tablespoon dried thyme

Method

Mix the ingredients together in a bowl, store in an airtight container or jar and add this versatile seasoning to perk-up chicken, seafood, chops and steak.

Sugar-Free Ketchup

Ingredients

170ml (6oz) tomato paste

2 tablespoons of onion powder

1 teaspoon garlic powder

1/2 teaspoon ground sea salt

150ml (5fl oz) apple cider vinegar

60ml (2fl oz) water

1/8 teaspoon of ground cloves

1/8 teaspoon cinnamon

1/8 teaspoon allspice

1/8 teaspoon pepper

Method

Place all the ingredients in a bowl and stir until smooth. Keep the ketchup in a glass jar in the refrigerator, ready to use.

Classic Vinaigrette

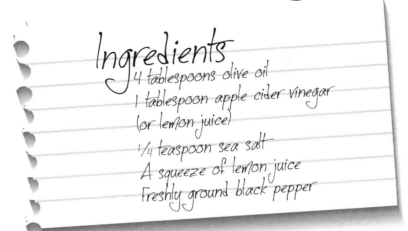

Ingredients
- 4 tablespoons olive oil
- 1 tablespoon apple cider vinegar (or lemon juice)
- ¼ teaspoon sea salt
- A squeeze of lemon juice
- Freshly ground black pepper

Method

Mix the ingredients together in a bowl or shaker before serving and use with fresh salads. You could substitute the vinegar for lemon juice, or try other varieties of vinegar instead.

Garlic Vinaigrette

Ingredients
- 4 tablespoons olive oil
- 1 tablespoon apple cider vinegar
- 1 clove garlic, crushed
- A squeeze of lemon juice
- ¼ teaspoon salt
- Freshly ground black pepper

Method

Mix all the ingredients together and store or use straight away.

Printed in Great Britain
by Amazon